The Belmont Addition

Carlie
Thank You
for Supporting My Dream.
Enjoy My Voice in print.
Marsha Akina Jordan 8/17/07

The Belmont Addition

by

Marsha Akins-Jordan

Bloomington, IN  Milton Keynes, UK

authorHOUSE®

AuthorHouse™
1663 Liberty Drive, Suite 200
Bloomington, IN 47403
www.authorhouse.com
Phone: 1-800-839-8640

AuthorHouse™ UK Ltd.
500 Avebury Boulevard
Central Milton Keynes, MK9 2BE
www.authorhouse.co.uk
Phone: 08001974150

First published by AuthorHouse 5/27/2007

ISBN: 978-1-4259-9808-0 (sc)
ISBN: 978-1-4343-0704-0 (hc)

Printed in the United States of America
Bloomington, Indiana

This book is printed on acid-free paper.

Editorial Notes: Even at the cost of grammatical rules, we have chosen not to capitalize the names satan and related names.

Unless otherwise indicated all Scripture quotations are from the Holy Bible. New International Bible Version. 1973, 1978, 1984 by the International Bible Society used by permission.

Scripture Quotations marked (KJV) are from the King James Version of the Bible.

Dedication

This book is dedicated to my father, the late R.J. Akins Sr., who taught me life survival skills, and my darling mother, Bobbie Jean (Fisher) Akins, who trained me in the ways of the Lord, and lived an exemplary lifestyle before me, and for always being there.

Contents

Preface

I have had the awesome privilege of walking with the author of this book through the foundational stages of her adult life up until this present moment. It has also been a blessing watching her cultivate, grow, and develop the gifts down on the inside of her. Her life is one that you can easily point out to others and say, "Follow her as she follows Christ".

One of the most remarkable things about Marsha Jordan is her uncanny ability to recall the exact details of her early childhood life through her college days. Random House Dictionary defines the word memory as a "mental capacity or faculty of retaining or recalling facts, events, impressions, or previous experiences." As you walk with Marsha through the days of her life, you will be struck with a sense of awe as she takes you directly into her world. She spares no detail and you can't help but laugh at her sense of humor as she describes teacher after teacher and incident after incident.

Gabrielle F. Simcock and Harlene Hayne in their article on *Multiple Measures of Memory: Continuities in Long-term Retention* gives us some insight into the realm of human memory. They state that… "Historically, there has been considerable debate about the nature of human memory development. Some researchers have argued that memory development occurs in a discrete stage-like manner while others have argued that memory development is a more smooth and continuous process"

After reading Marsha's account of her life, I believe that you will agree with me that she falls into the latter category. *The Belmont Addition* is not just another account of someone's life. It is an account of how a young lady gracefully walked through her life using all of the life skills taught her by her parents and the *Belmont* community. In writing this book, she dared to show her wounds so that others who stumble into similar circumstances can find their way out. I invite you to turn the page and begin a journey you will never forget.

Blanche Washington

Introduction

Small towns produce small ideas; small ideas never grow and mature into dreams, which eventually birth visions. This is the description of the small town mentality of Hugo, Oklahoma. In this place, your mind could easily become shackled by the unrealistic rules that governed the city.

When one wanted to disconnect from bondage, there was no scent of freedom. The winds of racism and prejudice were blowing in from the north, south, east, and the west collectively whispering, "This is the best that it is going to get". The single thought of what happened to chance was far removed from the picture. Employment was at an all time low, poverty covered the city with a coat of darkness, recreational areas were labeled "Whites only", the schools decorated their grounds with the words, "Unwed Mothers Not Welcome".

The only activities that ran rampant in the town was sex before marriage, innocent lives being captured from simple misunderstandings, and parents encouraging their children to leave the town in order to embrace a life of opportunity, freedom, and happiness.

Experience Marsha's childhood in the 1950's in a segregated town where everyone knew their place. Grow with her as she struggles with the cruel injustice of society. Feel the emotions of a young girl constrained by circumstances as she deals with the back lash and resentment that parallel the times. You are invited to share the trials, tears, triumphs, and the victorious outcome as you read her voice in print – "*The Belmont Addition*".

Acknowledgements

To God, my Redeemer, who empowered me to share my life in print.

To Blanche Washington, my big sister in the Lord, who caught a glimpse of this dream in the spirit realm, and with an anointed finger, became the Chief Editor of this book.

To Eva Wimbley, who assisted in the small details of the book.

Heartfelt thanks to Carolyn, Alexandra, and Nicholas Chingros for their support and words of encouragement.

A sincere thanks to my second grade student, Stetson Stallworth, for sharing with his parents, Stephanie,and Steve that I was writing a book, and for their enthusiasm which inspired me to pick my pen up and complete my book.

A special thanks to my wonderful husband, Darrel who encouraged me to follow my heart and write my life story. To my children, Kerwin, my first born, Daria, my only daughter , and to my baby, Darrel Jr.,

A heartfelt thanks to my best friend Sonya Young Cheltenham, who kept her hand in my back pushing me and telling me you, can do it!

Thanks to Angela Murray Olige for never tiring of listening and for being a great coach from start to finish.

Thanks to Vickie Alexander, Rosie Rogan, and Daria Jackson for the design of the book cover.

Chapter 1

THE BELMONT ADDITION

1   *The Belmont Addition*

Come and experience a lifestyle with me, a place where a community was established and built upon a group of hardworking, common Christian people. These people bound their love, gifts, and talents together to create an atmosphere conducive for raising children to become responsible individuals with respect, and character.

The fathers were the role models in exemplifying work ethics. The mothers were the trainers and teachers. The *Belmont Addition* was a place of obedience, respect, and love for all mankind. Hard work was the agenda of the day. This place had a code of ethics that was formulated by adults who laid a stake and held true to a vow that kept integrity, honesty, and commitment linked together.

Everyone in the city heard about the *Belmont* and the people who lived there, not because it was a place of status, but because it was a place of structure. It was noted not because it was a place of wealth, but because it was a place filled with people who were willing workers; not because it was a place of limitations, but because it was a place of loyalty.

98% of the families were from two parent homes, unlike the remainder of the city. Because of the strong family units, the children were raised to fear God, respect their elders, reverence the church house, school house, and the jail house.

Mr. Sam and Mrs. Cannie Bills had 16 children - the most children in the community. My parents were next in line, with 10 children. Because the Akins and the Bills were both dark in skin tone, people from the town often got them confused. But everybody in the *Belmont* knew the difference because we were all one big happy family. We were all so very close that every adult in the neighborhood could chastise and correct any behavior that was improper, and nothing was said. The exception was if the person who corrected you decided to tell your parents, you could count on getting another whipping. So we all learned how to become obedient children.

The *Belmont Addition* consisted of the Bills', Akins', Jackson's, Brown's, Scroggins', Fleek's, Gill's, Bostic's, Craft's, and the Garret's. All of the children in the community would meet under the street light under the hill to laugh, meddle and play. Those were the days of fun and getting to know each other and becoming a close-knit neighborhood. We did not fight each other, and we were able to tell each other the truth. During the summer we did not need a babysitter because each of us in our own family had to be responsible for our younger siblings. We were not allowed to visit each other when our parents were at work so we would yell out to each other and talk back and forth. We also had many chores to complete before our parents were scheduled to come home from work.

As soon as our parents arrived home, we were released from our duties to go play. We would all meet up and go pick blueberries, persimmons, plums, and apples. We were never hungry because everything grew in abundance in the *Belmont.* We would also go together to pick pecans so that we could have some money to help purchase some of the things that we needed for school.

We truly ate from the good of the land. We all even thought that commodities were a luxury. We had real cheese and had fun making grilled cheese sandwiches. We also put slices of cheese on our spam sandwiches which also came from the government commodities.

Every kid in the community went barefoot in the summer and we learned how to run and play on those hard dirt roads with all those huge rocks that filled the road without damaging our feet. We were also good at making tom-walker toys using pork and gravy cans, two clothes hangers that we stretched out to make them longer and then we would put two holes in the side of the cans and stick the wire hangers through them to walk on. Our brothers would make scooters and all kinds of fun things. On the weekends we would all play what the children now call "Hide and Go Seek" - we called it "Honey, Honey, Beep Bop Beep - I can't see ya - see ya - see - all ain't ready, holler Hi, Billy Goat".

On the week days we could only play until dusk because every kid in the *Belmont* knew that we had to be home before the street light came on, and if you were not, then everybody in the neighborhood knew that you got a whipping. You can imagine that we did not take any chances because if your mama called you by your first name and she had to call you twice and put the word "oh" in front of your name, that was your "for real" clue that you were going to get the beat down. If your father had to come looking for you, everybody in the hood was trembling in their boots because you knew that if your father had to come and get you, the same thing was going to happen to you.

When we were at play, we would sometimes just walk to the other street light down by the Ebenezer Baptist Church so that we could play with Kathy and her sister, Pumpkin. When we would pass by the church, we would get completely silent. When we walked by the jail house to and from school we would also become silent. When we saw the police car, we would not stare at the officer; we just got quiet and kept walking.

Our parents told us that the jail house was not made for cows and horses, and that if we went there, we would never be able to get out because they were not going to come and get us. We believed that report, so we avoided doing anything that would cause us to go to jail. We were told that you were not to steal and that if somebody had something for you, you did not have to steal it, nor did you have to ask for it because if someone had something for you they would give it to you.

We were taught to say " 'Mam, yes mam, and no 'mam", "sir, yes sir, and no sir" and that we were to always call an adult Mr. or Mrs. you called your aunts and uncles by uncle and aunt and their first name. We were taught to say "no thank you", even if you wanted what they were offering.

In the *Belmont,* we were taught to help anyone in need, respect widows, and help them clean their houses. We were taught to share with your siblings and anyone else who were in need. When we went to play, we just yelled out each other's name and if someone could not go play until they finished their chores, we automatically went over and helped them because we wanted to play with everyone in the community.

 When Halloween time came around, we would all get together and go Trick or Treating. We would get one of our parent's pillow cases to hold all the treats. When we all came home with all kinds of candy, we had the greatest time trading out and eating candy for days. Of course, we never got tired of eating candy.

At Christmas time we were more excited about having all kinds of foods and desserts that we could eat opposed to being concerned about what was under the tree. From past experience, we knew that we were going to get the same little black doll and our brothers were going to get bats for their baseballs. When the County Fair came to town, we had a blast. We used to all walk together and we would go on the hayrides, ride the Ferris wheel, and the Tilt the World ride. Those were truly days that I shall never forget.

In the *Addition*, we already knew that we were not going to be able to go to the doctor because our parents could not afford it, so our parents kept plenty of Vicks Vapor Rub, Castor Oil and SSS. If we had a tooth ache, we would go to the garden, chop up the garlic stem, chop the stem in a white rag and then tie the rag on the wrist where the side of your tooth was aching. If we had an ear ache, they would heat up the blessed oil, pour some in your ear and place some cotton from the mattress in your ear. The only good thing about being sick was you got the royal treatment from the siblings. They would gladly prepare your plate and bring it to your bedside because if you were too sick to eat everything on your plate, the person who brought the plate got to eat what was on your plate.

One thing that always made me sad in the *Belmont* was when it would rain. It seemed as though the rooms were smaller because we had to all stay inside. Our roof would leak so we had to place buckets strategically over different parts of our home to catch the water. The worst part were the roads. The roads in front of our houses were all dirt roads and it would take forever for the mud to dry up. In the meantime we had to walk barefoot and I never liked the way the mud felt in between my toes. My preference was to walk barefoot on the rocks instead of the mud.

In the **Belmont Addition**, there was no such thing as your parents missing work - they went to work every day. In the **Belmont Addition** we never missed school. In fact, we were the students who held the perfect attendance awards and we had to walk to and from school every day regardless of the weather. The children in the **Belmont** were not allowed to lie around in bed. You had a time to go bed, and a time to get up. You were up when the sun came out, and you had to have all your chores done before you were allowed to play.

Saturday was a hard work day. We had to get the water from the creek, heat the water in the two old black wash pots, and wash our clothes in the ringer washer, and then rinse the clothes in the number three tin tubs, hang all the clothes on the line; clean the house, mop the floors, clean out the kitchen cabinets, wash the walls, take the clothes in after they were dry and iron all your clothes for the week. Our chores also included raking the yard while the brothers mowed the yard. After everything was completed, we had about two hours of playing time before dusk dark.

On Sunday's we knew that we would go to Church all day. Even though we all had our own church homes, Mrs. Cannie would make everybody in the community learn an Easter and Christmas speech to say at the Ebenezer Baptist Church in the **Belmont Addition**. Every child in the community was a church kid. We had Mrs. Amos, who had a peg leg. She would teach us about the Bible stories. Then there was Elder Deary, who was a great teacher of the Word. He would put his loud speaker on and we would go and sit under his teachings for hours because we were taught to reverence the people and the things of God.

In the *Belmont* it was understood that everything you did, you did it together. We became this one great big happy family and we were known as the kids in the *Belmont Addition*. Therefore in my mind, heart, body, and soul, the *Belmont* is truly who I am. I still say today that because of the way that we were trained as children from the *Belmont Addition*, we did not have to join church to be taught how to love - we were taught it at home and in the community by leaders who showed us how to love.

We did not have to leave home to learn how to share with others because we were taught how to share with our siblings, relatives, and friends. We did not have to get married to learn how to take care of children - we were taught by helping our parents with our younger siblings and spending time with other family and friends. We did not have to join a church to learn how to obey leadership because we were trained how to be obedient to anyone who had the authority.

Welcome to the *Belmont Addition!*

Chapter 2

ON MY DADDY'S SIDE

2   *On My Daddy's Side*

"You shall not build a house, sow seed, plant a
vineyard, nor have any of these; but all your days
you shall dwell in tents, that you may live many
days in the land where you are sojourners."

JEREMIAH 35: 7

Truly, when I was just a little girl back in the fifties, I believed that life was great, and that "family" was the ultimate. I further believed that nothing else really mattered outside of family.

My ancestors were very poor, but they were so rich in love. Looking back over the earliest existence of my life, I must admit my father's family viewed life from a different perspective because of their upbringing. This behavior could have been due to the untimely death of their mother.

The primary responsibility of the older males in the Akins' family was to provide the food, shelter and clothing for their families. They were carefree about the things that were important to them. They actually did everything together from working, courting, marrying, gambling, lying, partying, and even going to church. If you saw one of them, I promise you were going to see many more.

The Akins' practiced behaviors such as "if you fought one, you had to fight them all". If one bought a car, the other one would buy one. If one got a job, they would make sure their employer hired some more of the family members. They would be friends today and then distant from each other tomorrow.

I believe it all started when my father's grandfather (my great grandfather), a one-armed white man, Jack Akins, settled in the ***Belmont Addition***. My great-grandfather married a young half-black and half-Indian girl who was young enough to be his daughter. She was only twelve years old when they married. Nine children were born to this union - Andrew, Edward, Jay, William, Jim, Dallas, Emma, Pinkie, and Maggie. My great grandmother was forewarned not to have any more children. As a result of the multiple births, she died at a very early age which left Grandpa Jack alone in a community of Blacks.

I truly believe Grandpa Jack was not ever given any trouble because his race did not consider him as one of them. All of his children were strong, big, tall, and hard workers. They were never late, they could work like mules and they were never sick. They smoked red Pall-Mall and Camel cigarettes, and they drank hard liquor. Everything that they did, they did it without a struggle.

Immediately after the death of my great-grandmother, Grandpa Jack married a young woman who bore him four more sons - Joe, Ennis, Leo, and Frank. Again, tragedy struck and his second wife preceded him in death. Now he has 13 children - ten sons and three daughters and no mother to teach or train them. At this point, they had to go for what they knew.

From the picture that was painted, to the younger generation, Grandpa Jack was a loving kind grandfather. The cousins, who knew him, remembered that he had one arm and that many years after his death his prosthesis was found in the roof of my grandfather's house.

My family was known to be fighters, gamblers, cussers, imitating kind of personalities. They were bold and daring, not hesitating to walk upon guns and knives. Their opponents were forced to kill them because they would not back down. As a matter of fact, you would never coward an Akins down. They would rather die than let another human get the best of them.

My female cousins were just as tough as my male cousins. They would stand toe-to-toe with any man and they always carried some type of weapon. The weapons ranged from a gun, knife, bottle, ice pick - you name it, they had it. The Akins' were so clannish that you would never find one of them alone.

The Akins' family was a male-dominant family. The women of the small town hated them, but they loved their money. Many of the women had babies by an Akins even though they were married men. My uncles and cousins were big womanizers. They always had a woman on the side. And you know how the news flash is in a small community - your business beat you home.

My grandpa lived until 1947 and never changed neighborhoods. The entire family remained in the **Belmont Addition** until it was cotton-picking time. My family, which consisted of my parents, grandparents, aunts, uncles, and cousins, would travel back and forth to Chandler, Arizona to pick cotton. They all traveled in caravans and would drive non-stop except for minimal restroom breaks. You would hear them bragging all the way about how good they were at driving. The families picked cotton until the season was over, and then once again, piled into those cramped-up cars and moved back to the *Belmont Addition.*

My Uncle Edward was my grandfather's brother. Uncle Ed and his wife, Aunt Jessie, had seven children. Their daughter Zelma died at an early age. Although they were our cousins, we called them aunt and uncle, i.e., Uncle Beck, Uncle Sammy, Uncle Rolyia, Aunt Helen, Aunt Thelma, and Aunt Lue Ella.

Uncle James (Becky) was tall, slender, and red in color. He was one of those kind that would cut you up and never stop smiling. Uncle Sammy was a huge, stout, robust man, with scary features. His voice was deep and frightening. He could whip any man with his bare hands. Uncle Roylia was tall, nice build, but he had huge hands and feet and was not afraid of anything. We always thought Uncle Roylia was cool because he was younger and more exciting. Uncle Roylia is presently serving as the Pastor of Hugo Chapel Baptist Church. Prior to this assignment, he served as the Hugo, Oklahoma Chief of Police.

Now Aunt Helen was quiet, but if you ever made her mad, she would jump you like a yellow jacket wasp nest that was disturbed. Aunt Thelma was not afraid of anything. She loved to drink beer and cuss, but she was no stranger to a real good fight. She was a provoker and would make you try and whip her. Aunt Thelma fought dirty, hitting with whatever was in sight. She also used a mean razor.

Last but not least, the one that everybody had a problem with was Aunt Lue. She was the family member that felt like everybody had to look up to her. She was the owner of all the one room shacks that we all had to live in when we went to Chandler to pick cotton. Aunt Lue talked down to all the family members, demanded her money, had her favorites out of the family, and did not mind letting the world know if she liked you or not. She drove a hard bargain and when you were on Lue Ella Baines' camp, she ran the whole show.

My grandfather's name was Jay and my grandmother's name was Maggie. They had five sons by the time my grandmother was 26 years old. My oldest uncle, A.C. (Uncle Son), was taken by my great-grandparents when he was young to raise him as their own. Due to this arrangement, he didn't get the opportunity to grow up with his brothers. He lived with my great-grandparents until he was 16 years old. The day Grandpa Will Comfort died, Uncle A.C. moved back home. My grandpa Jay was a happy man because he had yearned for his oldest son and all of his sons were together once again.

Uncle J. C. was labeled as the "rich" uncle. Uncle J.C. (Uncle Brother) wore a suit and a hat every day and kept a pocket full of money. He was tall and handsome and never made a difference between his nieces and nephews. Uncle J.C. always gave us money and was very comical.

Then there was my father, R. J., whom they called Black. My father was a quiet, reserved person. Although he was the smallest and the shortest, he held his own. My father was a mama's boy and stayed at home as long as he could. At the age of 21, Black married and had two children by his first wife – my sister Ruby Jewel, and R. J. Jr.

My Uncle J.B., whom we called Uncle Dido, was quiet and looked like Mama Mag's daddy, Will Comfort. Although Uncle J.B. did not bother anyone, he was always watching what was going on around him. He had his fair share of fun - he just did it differently.

The last of my uncles was Uncle W.L. We did not get a chance to meet him due to an untimely death. While working at a gravel pit, some of the gravel gave way and he was smothered to death beneath the rocks. They tried to dig him out, but to no avail. I have been told that he was a tall, dark man, who kept up a fuss between his brothers and sister-in-laws. He would convince his brother's wives to bake him all types of pies and then tell lies on his brothers. In spite of this, they said he was always the life of the party.

Uncle Andrew raised one son whom we called Honey Man. He was very good looking. They lived on the other side of town so we didn't get a chance to see him that much.

Uncle William was married to Aunt Lillie. They lived in the country and had two boys. Otis was the baby and was very smart in school. He made A's in every subject. He was also tall, and had big hands and feet.

Uncle William's second son, Charles, was a lot of fun. He drank a lot and went through life uncaringly. He also had two daughters - one of them they called Dimp (Mildred) and the other one, Ruby.

Aunt Pinkie had two girls – Emma (Mutt) whom she named after her sister, and Omie. Aunt Emma had a son named Willie who was big as well and we called him Big Dank. Aunt Maggie did not have any children.

The next set of relatives were the last four sons - Uncle Ennis, Leo, Joe and Frank. Ennis and Leo were murdered. Uncle Joe was a big red man who had a slight speech impediment. He kept to himself but could hold his own.

So this is my family on my daddy's side. Although the only ones who are left on my daddy's side of the family are Uncle J. B. (Dido) the last living sibling of my father. Uncle Sammy, Uncle Roylia, Aunt Helen, Aunt Thelma, Emma, (Mutt) Mildred (Dimp) and her sister Ruby. The generations of the Akins' family just keep on coming. The Akins name shall never die.

Chapter 3

ON MY MAMA'S SIDE

3   *On My Mama's Side*

*"Preach the word! Be ready in season and
out of season. Convince, rebuke, exhort,
with all longsuffering and teaching."*

2 TIMOTHY 4:2

Charley Davis Fisher Sr., my granddaddy, was a devout Baptist
preacher. He planted churches in Oklahoma, Texas, Kansas and
California. Granddaddy was tall, good looking, and he had Indian
written all across his face. He stood approximately 6 feet, 2 inches
tall and he had gold crowns on his front teeth. He weighed about
185 pounds and was a man of wisdom. It just seemed as though
he often times appeared to be self-righteous. He also raised his
children in the *Belmont Addition* and the Akins' were very fond
of him.

Charley Fisher preached, performed funerals, and married every
one of the Akins'. They respected him as a man of God and gave
him whatever they could to help him out. In spite of this, he felt
as though their children were not good enough to play with his
children.

My grandmother's name was Katie Kathryn Savannah (Rhodes)
Fisher. She was a tall, classy, beautiful lady. Grandmother loved

clothes and jewelry. She was a seamstress out of this world! She knew how to take a little and make a lot.

Grandmother was the oldest child of her mother and father's children. She would tell me how she would walk to church with her father for Sunday school and prayer services. She took pride in saying that she loved her mother, but she was really a daddy's girl.

Grandmother had eight children - Clarence James, Louis Drew, Dorothy Ola, Bobbie Jean, Charles Dale, Jr., Carl Edward, Joe Lewis, and Leonard. She also had one adopted daughter named Mattie, but to us she is affectionately called Aunt Mae. My grandmother taught her children the ways of the Lord. She would often gather them at her feet and teach them all the Bible stories. When they had church, her children would sing, play the organ, read the scripture, and pray. Granddaddy dreamt that before he died that five of his six sons would become pastors of churches. He lived to be 97 years old and saw his dream become a reality.

Grandpa was a man of discipline. He said exactly what he meant and meant exactly what he said. His children did not break his rules. The irony behind my mama's side and my daddy's side was the fact that my grandparents allowed my father to marry their baby girl, but would not allow Uncle Son, my daddy's oldest brother, to marry my mother's only sister. Instead, they sent her to California to live with her brother. This historical family fact is what made me want to get a better understanding of my family on my mama's side.

My father married my mother when she was 15 years old. A year later granddaddy and grandmother Fisher all moved lock, stock, and barrel to Coffeeville, Kansas. My mother was the only one of her family members left in the **Belmont Addition**. Mother had three aunts who lived in the city - Aunt Trealious, Aunt Clyde, and Aunt Lillian. Aunt Trealious was the town's beautician. Aunt Clyde was the town's barber. Between the two of them, they had a large clientele and were doing very well.

The one thing I could not figure out was why they never had anything to do with the Akins' side of the family. We were their oldest sister's grandchildren, but they acted as though we were from another planet. They were not really nice to my parents.

As time went on, we never heard from any of my mother's family, except uncle C.D. who was my favorite Uncle. Uncle C.D. could sing and preach. He was tall and good looking. He had a way with people when he entered the room you knew he was somebody. He married the cutest little wife - my Aunt Vivian. When Aunt Vivian hugged you, you felt like like a teddy bear. When she offered you something to eat, she made it look good as well as taste good. My cousins Roger, Joan, and Ginger always came to Hugo to visit. We had so much fun - we would walk downtown to the Cowlings grocery store with our *proper* cousins from Kansas.

Mother had another brother who married a lady whose name was Italian Teresa and we called her Aunt I. T. She was from a small country town outside of the Hugo city limits. We used to love it when Uncle Louis and his family came to town from Wichita Kansas. Our cousins, Louis Don, Gregory Dean, Karen Denise, and Myrtle Kaye were very proper and we were the rowdy country cousins. But life was good and at least we had an opportunity to spend time with two sets of our cousins on my mama's side. The sad part of the commentary is that my mother had only one sister and my father did not have any sisters. Needless to say, we longed to meet our only Aunt.

Thank God for the kind of mother we had!! Mother had a family picture of her parents and siblings and she talked about them as she pointed each one of them out. We didn't meet mother's only sister - Aunt Dorothy, until we were almost grown. Aunt Dorothy lived in California and she never came to visit us while we were little because she too was raising her children. Aunt Dorothy had four children - two daughters, Patricia, Carolyn Jean, who she named after my mother, Henry Jr., and Charles. They were one year apart in age.

Mother had the opportunity once a year to visit her parents and her siblings during the week of the 4th of July. Mother could not afford to take off from her job each year for a week so the Glove Factory where she was employed closed the plant down for the entire 4th of July week. Mother's family scheduled their family reunions once a year during that time. Since mother could not afford to take all eight of us with her, we had to stay home with Daddy.

We were glad that Mother had the chance to travel to many states where each of her siblings lived and to spend time with her family. We were also glad when she returned because Daddy could not cook. Daddy was also strict about everything. All we had was a picture of Mother's family and the memories that she shared with us. We thought that the Fisher's had it all together.

Uncle Clarence James was my mother's oldest brother. He was a quite man but when he opened his mouth he spoke words of wisdom. He had nice diction and he carried himself like a man of honor and distinction. He always seemed to know where he was going and how he was going to get there. Uncle Clarence had several children as well but getting an opportunity to know them all was a challenge because they lived on the West Coast. You can imagine how excited we were when we met them the very first time.

Uncle Joe was the rich uncle who excelled in everything he touched. He often shared the story about how he loved cars and that at the age of 16 he drove my grandparents to Los Angeles, California. The remarkable thing about this trip was that the car he drove belonged to him.

Uncle Joe married my Aunt Betty who has since gone on to be with the Lord. My Uncle Joe and my Uncle C.D. married two sisters - Aunt Vivian and Aunt Betty. We really felt special when mother would show us the pictures of our Aunts. They looked like twins to us.

Uncle Joe and Aunt Betty had three children – Diane, who was the oldest, Steve, and Dale. Uncle Joe was the owner and operator of a full service gas station while he and Aunt Betty lived in California. He later got a job with General Motors and became a traveling executive. We did not get a chance to meet his children until much later in our lives because of the extensive traveling that Uncle Joe's job required of him.

Uncle Leonard was the youngest child. He was only a year older than my sister Bernice, and my two cousins - Aunt Dorothy's daughter, Pat, and Uncle Clarence's daughter, Verba. Uncle Leonard was quiet but cool. When he visited us, he would get in the trenches with us. We could share ideas and stories and he always had an ear to listen. We finally had cousins that were younger than we were Angie, and Anthony. Aunt Arlene, Uncle Leonard's wife, was so very pretty to us and she could really sing. We had a great time with them.

Uncle Carl always acknowledged all of his Kinfolks no matter who they were. He was proud of his family so of course everybody loved Uncle Carl. He was always a happy-go-lucky person and full of fun. He had a "bossy uncle" personality, but he was also very understanding. Uncle Carl had no problem telling the truth on you and himself. Uncle Carl died at the age of 48. The one lasting memory that I will always cherish is that Uncle Carl performed the wedding ceremony for Darrel and me.

When I was born, my grandparents moved to California in 1955 and granddaddy planted a church there and they lived there until they both died. I really wanted to find out what was this deep dark secret about my mama's side of the family - why was it so hard for them to connect with us? Why did they act like we were not related to them? I went on a mission to find out, and after I got in the water, the tides began to gather around my waist, then it moved toward my shoulders, and I swam back to safety and hated I found out what I did.

Over all, our families were different, and yet they were alike in so many ways. The spirit of rejection always seemed to raise its ugly head when I had to deal with family. Although my families from both sides were loving people, they seemed to share some of the same type of behaviors.

The family members who are still alive on my mama's side are Clarence James, Louis Drew, Dorothy Ola, Bobbie Jean – (my Mother), Joe Lewis, Leonard, and Aunt Mattie Mae. Grandmother Katie has two sisters who are still living - Aunt Clydia, the barber of Hugo, and Aunt Essie. These are the relatives on my mama's side.

Chapter 4

THE LITTLE GIRL INSIDE OF ME

4   *The Little Girl Inside of Me!*

*"The streets of the city shall be full of boys
and girls playing in the streets"*

ZECHARIAH 8:5

For as long as I can remember I have always wanted to go to school. I loved people and I enjoyed learning. I wanted to be in a place where I could show off my talent while others looked on in amazement. We were living in Chandler, Arizona at the time. I was four years old and my sister, Debra, was two. Mother had prepared breakfast for all of us - Bernice, Arbrey, Charley, Kenneth, Debra, and me. Daddy had gone to work, and mother was taking Debra and me to the sitter's house.

Mother stopped at the local grocery store to purchase our snacks for the day. She left the key in the ignition and the motor was still running while she went into the store. I thought this was the perfect time to teach Debra the ABC song. Well, Debra had other things on her mind. She slid under the driver's seat and put the drive shaft in reverse and our car collided into the owner of the store's car. I was the oldest and remember crying while blood was streaming down my face from a bloody nose and lip.

At the same time, Debra was cool as a cucumber acting like she could not understand why I was yelling and screaming. I can still remember the puzzling look of fright on my mother's face. She did not know if we were okay, and she realized that it was the owner's car that was damaged.

Mother cleaned me up as best she could and took us on to the sitter's house. I remember the sitter oh so well. She was a tall, slim lady. She had a quiet demeanor and was a preacher's daughter, and she was also a newly wed. Her father was a Church of God in Christ preacher, who lived in Phoenix, but he pastored one of the local churches in Chandler.

Mother dropped us off at Mrs. Vanley's and scurried on to work. She was driving daddy's car. It was a green Pontiac and the fender was hanging off from Debra's accident. My mother was quite the mother to have been only 28 years old with 6 children and she had miscarried one in between Debra and me.

Mother was a domestic worker and cleaned Mrs. Hooks home for ten dollars a week. While she had to leave her two younger children for someone else to keep, go home to a one room shack where our only seating was on the bed with no bathroom, no kitchen, no closets, no windows and no doors - just one way in and the same way out - we were just dirt poor. But because we were with family, it didn't matter. We never thought about it.

My cousin Sharon Lue and I would argue all the time. She could never pronounce my name correctly - she would call me Washa Jo instead of Marsha Jo. She would tell me, "Washa Jo, you can't come in we's house", and I would tell her "you can't come in our house either". Our older sisters, Ruby Jewel and Sharon's sister Thelma Jean would laugh at us because we really thought our one room was really a house. In spite of the hot weather and the scorching sand, we still had fun with each other in the evening after the sun had gone down.

We used to play around the camp and all kinds of strange things would go on at night. There was this lady named Nell and she had a boyfriend that used to beat her every time he would come home drunk. We would feel so sorry for her, but we did not know what to do. We used to hate to see him coming when he would come home drunk. At other times we would go around to Mr. Leonard's side. He used to always have his window cracked and we could see inside his house when we would run and play. He would have a stocking cap on his head and he would wear his long johns to bed. He would always go to bed early. My brother Kenneth was so bad - he made up a song and had all of our cousins sing this song: "Mr. Leonard with his long stringy drawers hanging down" - if mother would have known that we were doing that, she would still be beating us now. So make sure that you never say what your children will not do.

The summer went by rapidly. We were always out in the hot sun playing because it was just as hot inside. We used to walk all in the neighborhood stores. On the way to the store was a small cave that we would hide in and play, and keep cool for the long trip back home.

My father worked so hard, but he was also a gambler. Sometimes he would work in the cotton patch all week long and lose his entire pay check on a croaker sack to his family members. My mother never told us their business - she loved daddy, and taught us by example how to love him, but my older brother always wanted more. He never could quite understand why our parents continued to have children because he felt like we would never have anything. He felt like life would have been great if mother would have just had my oldest sister Bernice and him.

My sister Bernice was quite different. She always wanted to make sure we had enough. She would care for us and never complain. Bernice would often times go lacking herself just to make sure we were all happy.

I still could not understand why our grandmother, who lived in California, never came to see us, but I guess if she had come where was she going to sleep? So that side of the family became just a picture in our minds. We longed to know the other side of our family but we just kept them in a safe place in our heart and left them alone.

We had Mama and Papa Akins. Papa Jay loved his children and his grandchildren. He was a quiet kind man, but if you wanted to ruffle his feathers, just bother his grandchildren and he would absolutely lose it. Mama was always fussing about something, but deep inside we knew that was the only way she knew how to show love. As long as she was fussing, we would always have something to laugh about because she was so comical.

I can remember the last time we had to go to Mrs. Vanley's - mother dropped us off and again she had to scurry off to work. The one thing that I recognized more now than ever, was she lived across the street from a big red school house. I could not believe my eyes as I watched the children playing. The girls' pony tails were flopping as they jumped rope and the boys were playing football. Some were playing kick ball and others were swinging in the swings while others were going down the big silver tin slide. The teachers all stood in strategic places as they watched the children play as if they were correctional officers. The sound of laughter and screams of joy were all around me and the colors of pastels were in my view.

I can still hear "ring around the roses - a pocket full of posies" as the girls all sang in harmony. The school yard was huge and the grass was nowhere to be seen - only sand everywhere. My mind went back to when I was teaching Debra the ABC song. I wondered what they had learned in the classroom, was learning fun, were the teachers like mothers or were they strict? Did the children raise their hands or did they yell the answers out. I thought school must be great, but what do I do? How can I get over the fence to go into the classroom? I often wondered, "Will I ever be able to go to school?" If so, what is school like? I could even imagine only in part, but whatever it was or whatever it wasn't, I still wanted to go to school.

My older siblings were able to go to school and they seemed to be excited about whatever books they were reading. They always seemed to be working on some kind of work every day when we came home form Mrs. Vanley's. Then I was awakened from my day dream to the saddest sound that I had heard all day – it was the sound of the school bell ringing alerting the children that it was time for them to stop playing and go back into the classroom.

I looked over toward the school and I saw the girls and boys run into their lines as though they were in the branch of the service waiting for their teachers to march them into their classrooms. Then Mrs. Leona called my name softly, saying to me "Marsha, it's time for you to come inside".

I CAN STILL REMEMBER PRESSING MY FACE INTO THE CHAIN LINK FENCE, AND THOUGHT TO MYSELF, IF I COULD JUST GO TO SCHOOL. At that very moment I believe that this was the turning point of the little girl inside of me wanting to come out. This ambition was impregnated into my spirit and the enemy knew that he was going to cut the umbilical cord of education at an early age to block my dream   (to go to school). Exactly 11 years later, the one thing that I desired the most was taken from me – my pursuit of education.

Chapter 5

1ST GRADE
MS. JESSIE D. BOREN

5   *1st Grade Ms. Jessie D. Boren*

*"And he sat down, called the twelve, and
said to them, if anyone desires to be first, he
shall be last of all and servant of all."*

MARK 9:35

There is something about "first" when you are always last. First grade sounds real good. I was so excited I almost burst out with happiness. I had my 7–days-a- week panties that were yellow, pink, blue, purple, white, and green. At the right hand corner were embroidered the words Monday, Tuesday, Wednesday, Thursday, Friday, Saturday, and Sunday. I also had five new dresses with huge beautiful bows that daddy would tie into the prettiest bow that would stay all day.

I looked at my new bobbie socks and my new pair of black and white oxfords - just waiting for me to put them on for the "first" day of school. Mother had my hair curled in those Shirley temple curls with the cute bangs in front. Mother tied my hair up before I went to bed so that the curls would stay in place. I was so excited I knew that I would not be able to sleep, but I did not tell mother. Finally about midnight on the Sunday night before school was to start, I finally felt my eyelids get heavy and I went fast asleep.

I remember waking up to the smell of fried bacon, sausage, rice, scrambled eggs, homemade biscuits and apple butter. It is the first day of school! I sprang out of bed and dressed myself in my new red and green checked dress. And of course daddy tied the most beautiful bow in the back of my dress so it would stay tied all day long. My hair was like that of satin curly waves. My face was shining like new money from the Vaseline which was our lotion substitute.

This was the first time in my life that I felt pretty. I was so excited I could not eat. I heard the dimes drop on the table as daddy counted out our 5 dimes each so that we could eat lunch at the school canteen which consisted of chocolate or white milk in the carton, five cookies - either chocolate and vanilla or just vanilla. The cookies reminded me of tires on a bicycle - only smaller. They also had hot dogs and greasy sloppy joe's, but who cared - at least we had food to eat and besides, Mrs. Bostic was the head cook, and we knew her Thanksgiving menu was going to be great.

I gathered together my new pencils - the real fat ones. One of them was blue and the other one was red. I also had my big red writing tablet that had the face of an Indian chief on the front of the tablet. I was finally getting ready to live out my dream of "if I could just go to school".

Kenneth and I hurried to the bus stop to catch up with Elroy, Larry, Lewis, and Franklin Bills; our cousins Shirley Ann, and Sharon Lue, then Ray, Sue, Betty, Mary Louise, whom we called Pete and Lela Faye whom we called (Monkey). Then there were the Jackson's, Verna Jean, Claudester, Linda Faye, and Jackie Wayne, and last but not least, Pumpkin and Cat - all from the *Belmont Addition!*

We gathered at the corner and waited under the telephone pole. We were all waiting to see what each one had on that was new. We all thought we were cleaner than a whitty fish! At last we see the big yellow school bus coming down the hill. Kenneth and his friends would always yell out, "Here comes the B U S". We scrambled to get our school supplies in our hands so that we could get on the bus. When the bus driver pulled the big yellow bus up and opened the doors, I had no idea that the bus driver, Mr. C. V. Gage, would become the grandfather of my first child.

When I got on the bus, there were two young guys sitting quietly on the bus. I later found out that they were Mr. Gage's sons, Wesley and Travis. Well, you know I love to talk and my voice was very loud and I was always out of my seat.

On the first day of school, Mr. Gage had to reprimand me as he looked through the mirror asking me to sit down. My question was – "out of all the kids on the bus, how did he know my name?"

The bus finally pulled up in the back of the school house – good old Booker T. Washington. Sharon Lue, Lela Faye, Kathy, Jackie Wayne, Franklin Don and I went to find our first grade class. Our classroom was the first door on the right hand side of the school. When we entered into the classroom, we were greeted by our first grade teacher, Ms. Boren. She was standing at the door to greet us with a hearty "Good Morning".

We all scrambled to a seat thinking that we would be able to sit wherever we wanted to sit. Ms. Boren immediately took charge of her classroom and gave us the rules for that day.

1.   Come into the classroom quietly.

2.   No talking to your neighbor.

3.   Raise your hand before blurting out.

4.   Take out your pencils and Big Chief Tablets.

5.   Wait for the teacher to assign your seat.

We all knew that this teacher meant business and she was not to be played with - and this was only the first day of school! Ms. Boren stood 5 feet and 8 inches tall. She wore her hair in a page boy style. Her bangs came to her eyebrows and they were tucked neatly in a straight line on her forehead. Her hair in the back was tucked neatly under at the base of her neck. She wore a pure white blouse that had a beautiful bow tied in the front that swung down in the center of her chest.

Ms. Boren had on a red polyester skirt that came past her knees and flared at the bottom making a complete circle. Her perfume smelled like peppermint with a dash of ginger mixed with it. Her teeth were small in the front and white as the ivory under an elephant's trunk. She wore small wire frame glasses that looked like mirrors that were glued to her eyes and were clear as crystals as though she had scrubbed them all morning. Her fingers were long and slender with a single coat of clear nail polish evenly distributed on each fingernail. that looked as though they were freshly painted. Her legs looked like tooth picks that were poured into her grandma black lace up shoes that looked as though the heels could be about a ½ inch tall. Her feet were small and dainty, and extremely narrow and looked to be about a size 7 or 71/2.

Ms. Boren rarely smiled, but her spirit was two-fold, kind on one hand, but on the other hand, it was that of authority. I summed up my first grade teacher for the first time on the first day of school. I must admit there was something very intriguing about her, and deep down inside I thought I kind of liked her.

Ms. Boren immediately went into her daily routine of singing the song that she taught us. The words to this song were:

> **We are all in our places**
> **With sun- Shinning faces**
> **For this is the way**
> **To start our new day.**

Well you know I was too much of a talker to be a singer. I was loud so you can imagine me singing louder than everyone else and off key as well. I cannot stress to you how happy I truly was to be in the first grade.

Ms. Boren's classroom was very cheerful. It was painted a real light green with ABC letters placed on the wall. Just above the black board there was a reading chart with a picture of Spot, the dog. She had flip charts that had the story of Dick and Jane on them. I thought "School is great, and learning really is fun!"

To the south of the room were three rows of windows where we could look out and see the beautiful landscaping and the surrounding neighbor's home. Our desks were wooden and we were able to slide into them from one side of the desk. There was a pencil identation on the top of the desks to place our pencils so that they would not drop on the floor.

I looked around my new classroom and I ended up sitting beside a girl whose name was Ruth Denise Burris. She and I became instant best friends. The rest of the morning all you could hear was the ABC's and the story – "See Spot run, run Spot run". The repetition of counting 1-2-3-4-5-6-7-8-9 and 10 over and over was more than I expected. I must admit, all I really wanted to do was go to school!

At last we had an opportunity to go out for morning recess. We had so much fun that when we heard the bell for us to come back inside it was the saddest sound we had heard all day.

Well, we made it through the school year and at the end of the year we were all wondering if we were going to be promoted to the second grade. Finally we made it to the last day of school of the first grade.

May 22, 1962 finally came around and we could not wait to look at our report cards. What a great fun year even though it was a hard year, we learned so much. We all immediately looked on the back to see if we were promoted to the second grade and we all shouted with glee as we saw "PROMOTED TO 2ND GRADE".

When we all received our report cards you should have seen our entire class - running, hugging, laughing, and some were really crying but we all had been promoted to second grade - WOW!

Chapter 6

2ND GRADE
MS. HAZEL ROGERS

6   *2nd Grade Ms. Hazel Rogers*

*"The second is: Love your neighbor as yourself. There
is no other commandment greater than these."*

MATTHEW 12: 31

Summer is over and today is the first day of school. We have all
grown a few inches and are anticipating going to school to enter
into another year with another teacher. But at least we still have
the same classmates. Second grade was not as exciting to me as
first grade was. Our new teacher's name was Ms. Hazel Rogers.
She was pleasantly plump, a tall lady; she had huge fat jaws that
made her look as though she had the mumps year round. She did
not smile often and she had moles scattered on her face and neck;
her fingers were short and she had chubby feet and ankles. They
looked as though they were swollen all the time. Ms. Rogers did
not wear any jewelry and she wore her hair pulled all the way from
her face in a bun in the back.

On the first day of school, Ms. Rogers wore a long red and white
checkered dress. The dress had a square collar and she wore a
beautiful white sweater that she allowed to hang off her shoulders.
She never put her arms through the sleeves.

Ms. Rogers really had a "no nonsense" attitude when it came to
playing and joking. I remember her room was kind of dull. She

worked a lot from the board with a pointer that she used daily as well as constantly. Ms. Rogers would take the palm of her hand and beat you in your back if you missed a question in her classroom, or if you talked or snickered in her classroom.

Ms. Rogers did not appear to have any favorite students - she just wanted everybody to do what she asked them to do. Ms. Rogers was known by the sardines that she used to eat from the can with Louisiana Hot Sauce and her juicy red delicious apples that she had on her desk every day. She told us that an apple a day would keep the doctor away.

I know she was just trying to teach us a nursery rhyme because if you were sick in our home you were not going to go the doctor, but I still loved how the apples she had on her desk made the room smell. Besides, our teachers knew that our parents were common laborers and that at Christmas we would get an apple and I would think that it would take more than eating an apple once a year to keep the doctor away.

There was nothing exciting about Ms. Rogers. I am sure, however, that she was a good teacher - she just did not seem to have the intestinal fortitude it took to motivate children to learn. I must admit I did well in my studies, but I really did not enjoy my second grade as much as I did my first year.

Although our older siblings always had the same teachers before we made it to that particular grade, they never voiced an opinion about Ms. Rogers. I do not know if it was because she was mean, or if she did not like school or if she had the burnouts, but I actually cannot remember ever feeling whole in her classroom - everything was so stringent. There were no fun times and the lessons seemed long and boring. That was not to say that 2nd grade might have been a difficult year for all of us, but we continued to do what was expected of us.

In my heart of hearts, I was really ready for the school year to end. At recess, all of us were our most happiest. We would swing in the swings and slide down the slide. I was always very daring, but the memories of my second year in school were not as fond.

Everyday at lunch time Ruth and I would go over to her house for lunch and her mother, Ms. Myrtle, always had really good food for us to eat. We would sometimes skip over to Ruth's house and then we would run back quickly so that we could have a few minutes left to play at recess. Being able to get away at lunch time was a secret that only Ruth and I shared.

Life was just so great - I had my best friend and we had so much fun together. Before we knew it, the school year was once again winding down. I spent so many nights with Ruth until I became a part of their family.

I can still remember Eva, who allowed me to ride her bike unconditionally, and how she used to love The Supremes; she would read the Jet magazines constantly. Her sister, Rosie Bell, would wear a head scarf tied around her head. I can still remember how every strand of hair would be in place when she took it off. I thought she was very pretty, but she would always get disgusted with Ruth and me because all we wanted to do was play. We would try to wash the dishes and she would run us out of the kitchen because she claimed we were just going to half do them. Ruth and I would gladly leave out and keep playing.

Ruth's oldest sister always gave me a hard time, but I always knew that it was done in love. She would always have me scratch her scalp and then she would decide when Ruth and I could go play.

Carrie was always the life of the party. She would scare us out of our minds telling us old wives' folk tales and then she would laugh and play with us for hours.

I truly enjoyed my time with the Burris'. After all these years, we are still family. Ruth and I became inseparable. At the end of the year all our classmates became real fearful because they did not know if we were going to pass or fail and the most embarrassing thing that could happen to any student at Booker T. Washington School was to flunk your class. As a matter of fact, it was almost unheard of to flunk a grade.

Although we were young, we understood the seriousness of completing our class work, never missing an assignment and always working our hardest. Not promoting a child because he or she could not complete their assignment was just part of the black culture. Ruth and I were confident that this was not going to happen to us. We knew what was expected from our parents as well as our teachers and believed they all wanted what was best for us. They pushed us with everything that was within them.

Our teachers had no problem whipping, chastising or even criticizing us. Most of our whippings were from not turning in our assignments or even missing an answer after they had taught the lesson including missing a spelling word. They gave us a night to complete the assignment, and if you missed a spelling word, you were given licks in your hand. You were taught respect for your elders and you never talked back. Whatever the teacher asked you to do, you did it and you did it without an attitude. The one thing that we enjoyed in second grade was Chapel. We would all stand up and recite the Pledge of Allegiance, sing a song, and read a scripture verse. Each class would then have an opportunity to perform for the entire student body. We were glad to go to the assemblies because we could sit with our friends, but usually we would end up in trouble. If the teachers caught us talking, we would get a whipping when we got back to the classroom.

Our second grade year was more of an introduction into the real world of school and it hurt, but we made it through. At the end of the year, we were once again so happy because all of us had been passed to the third grade. Once again we were one big family and we loved being in the same class together every year.

I must admit I was glad when the second year of school was over and we had the summer to play in the ***Belmont Addition***. We all walked home together on the last day and sang our little theme song "Schools out - schools out - teachers let the student's out". Boy, were we glad!

Chapter 7

3RD GRADE MS. VELASKA HUNT

7   *3rd Grade Ms. Veleska Hunt*

*"And God has appointed in the Church, first
Apostles second Prophets, third Teachers".*

1ST Corinthians 12:18

We have all been promoted to the third grade now and we really
feel like upper classmen although it's only third grade. Our new
teacher this year is none other than Ms. Velaska Hunt. Ms. Hunt
was a quiet, even tempered person. She had long cold black hair
that came to the base of her neck. Her face was shaped like the
letter "v". Her eyes were cold black and she had medium sized lips.
Her nose was slightly pointed and she had a habit of hunching up
her shoulders. It was like it was an involuntary movement.

She had the cutest shape out of all the teachers in my school. Her
legs were pretty and smooth. When she walked, she took quick
short steps. She always had her hands on her hips when she would
give a directive. She was very kind, but Ms. Hunt did not play and
would whip you without thinking about it.

I personally feel that she was more than a teacher, she was a born
educator. She did not expect anything except perfection out of
every one of her students. There was no such word in Ms. Hunt's
classroom that you could not do something. She said you could,

and she made sure you did. If you had to stay there all day, you were going to get it right.

I remember that third grade was a difficult year for me. I was able to figure out with ease the first and second grade class work, but in third grade I had to think about it because the required skills changed on me. This is the first grade that we were introduced to the three "T's" telling time, tying your shoes, and times tables. Wow! What a change from counting to 100 and reading about Spot, Dick, and Jane.

One day I was in class and Ms. Hunt gave a directive that we were no longer going to print but we were going to write cursive. She had trained us by way of modeling on the board and utilizing our worksheets. Well, I always loved to write - so that was not my issue. My problem was the recess bell was going to ring and I wanted to go out to recess so I printed the work. Ms. Hunt checked over all our writing and she came to the playground and told me to come back in the classroom and write the assignment. Well, I went back in and all I did was hook the letters together. Mrs. Hunt called me in again and told me to erase it and write the assignment. This time I erased some of it and wrote it correctly. She called me in the third time and she whipped me real good. Every since that day, I became the master writer. Nobody could beat me writing. I would take pencil and paper out to recess daring and challenging anybody to out-write me. Now you know, there was not one to be found including the boys that could out write me.

My next dilemma was, I could not understand how a quarter after the hour and a 9 before the hour could both be called a quarter before and a quarter after. When I finally figured it out, my classmates were sick of me because I would raise my hand and blurt the answer out before Ms. Hunt could call my name.

Thirdly I had a problem tying my shoe; however I was the best rope jumper - that is until my shoes came untied. I tried to figure out after I made the first loop what to do next - this is when I decided not to be angry with Ms. Hunt's niece, Kathryn Ann. Kathryn came from out of nowhere. She wasn't with us in the first or second grade. Since she could read, she was promoted to the third grade. Well, you know I was hot. I told her out loud at a time when Ms. Hunt was in ear distance, because I wanted her to hear what I had to say about the matter. I said, "Kathryn you are not that smart, you only got skipped to the third grade because your Aunt is the third grade teacher".

Kathryn Ann truly loved me and wanted to be my friend. She was always hanging around Ruth and me because she wanted to be close to me. I must admit I did kind of like her. I just felt like she was threatening my space. I was supposed to be the smartest kid in the class, not the teacher's niece. I must admit that I had inherited my head full of beautiful hair and my cold black complexion from my father and Kathryn thought this was the ultimate.

You know how kids that are related to teachers seem to always have more than enough and kids whose parents are common laborers seem to never get enough. Well, Kathryn Ann started out by sharing with me. I tell you my readers; there is no greater way to win the heart of a person than to become a giver. Soon afterwards, Kathryn wanted to take my pony tails down every day and re-comb my hair. I could care less about hair, it was long to my shoulders and my face had no blemishes. I just thought it would be prettier if it was as brown as Kathy's.

At recess, because I was so good at jumping rope, I would always be the choice jumper. I always ordered red hot - I never wanted warm which was slow and I never wanted medium which was not fast enough. When I ordered red hot, even Booley, Terry, and Jimmy would help throw the rope because everybody wanted to get me out. I was so good - I could criss-cross, turn around, touch the ground, come back up, and never miss a beat.

One day when I came out of the jump rope ring, my shoes were untied. I stooped down to tie them but to no avail, I could not do it. So I called Kathryn Ann over. Now allow me to share with you a pet peeve of mine - I could never stand to be fronted off. In other words, "don't try to embarrass me in front of a crowd". Well, Kathryn Ann came over and I whispered to her and asked her to tie my shoe. After all, she wanted to be my friend and I figured that's what friends are for. My friend Ruth would have never fronted me - she would just tie my shoe no matter how many times. Well Miss Kathryn Ann decided to tell everybody that I could not tie my shoe. I lost it - after all, I had just won the biggest jump rope tournament of the recess hour. I told her I don't need you to tie my shoe and that I could tie my own shoe and I wasn't going to be her friend.

I sat there for what seemed like hours trying to tie my shoe. I must admit I felt so bad within myself realizing that at eight years old I could not tie my shoes. But I tell you, that day I truly learned what friendship meant. I learned that it was not you trying to buffalo people to do what you want them to do. It was not trying to show the world that you are better than everyone else, nor was it being prideful because you can do a job better than anyone else. Rather, it was a give and take situation - always preferring others before yourself.

In spite of my hurting Kathy's feelings, she came back over to me, stooped down to where I was and said "I am not mad at you - I want to teach you how to tie your own shoes so that if I am not around and you are in a place by yourself, you can tie your shoes just as good as you can read, write, jump rope, and play jacks". She said, "Marsha you are smart, you can do this". That same day I was a changed individual. I learned how to tie my own shoe and Kathryn, Ruth, and I became the threesome. All in all, the change was great.

After Kathy and I became friends, she invited me over to their house to spend the night. They had a brick and half siding on their house. The carpet was plush and off-white. Their bathroom was just absolutely like it was shipped in from one of those home magazines. I remember the pink tile that overlaid the walls and a long mirror from wall to wall to see yourself. Kathryn Ann's room was so pretty and dainty. She had a beautiful light oak wood bed with a dresser to match. The dresser was oval shaped and she had the cutest little bench that she could sit on and comb her hair. She had a silver comb and brush set to match, but Kathryn's hair was very short and it was filled with tiny little braids that were hooked to each other to make her hair look longer than it really was.

Kathryn had every color of nail polish and her closet was filled with clothes and more clothes. I thought to myself - she is rich. She had this beautiful emerald green coat that I kept trying on over and over again, longing to have one just like it. Kathryn never blinked at the things that she had. We were so opposite, she wanted a friend and I wanted things. She could care less about the clothes, the coat, and her room. She was an only child and there were too many kids where I came from. We had great fun in her room. She would take my hair down and comb it in all kinds of styles. She would paint my fingernails. I remember telling her, "You better get that white fingernail polish off my nails. My fingers are too black for that color". However, she thought it was absolutely pretty.

I must admit we had so much fun that I really thought she was a nice person, and deep down inside I felt really bad for the mean things that I had said about her. One day Kathy and I got into an argument after school and we caught up with the instigators, Booley and Terry. We were both trying to tell our side of the story and get them to agree with us or take sides. All they did was laugh at us all the way home. Kathy and I were so mad with them. We walked on the opposite side of the street until we got to Kathryn Ann's grandmother's store.

Kathryn Ann's grandmother's name was Mrs. Josephine Hunt. When she heard that Kathy and I were mad and bickering with each other, she came out of the store and said, "Now Kathryn and Marsha, you all stop this right now. You all are friends and I don't want to hear another word about you all being mean to each other". She called me into the store and told me to get what I wanted. Back then those big yellow banana bite kits were the candy. I was able to pick that candy free of charge! I still had a ways to go to get to the *Belmont Addition*. Kathryn and I still laugh about how my attitude changed when I got that candy. She said I walked home with that banana bite in my mouth and was happy all the way.

Kathryn and I have remained best of friends since third grade and I can honestly say that we have never had another argument about anything. We have always been able to pick back up where we left off although she moved to Bakersfield, California at the end of our eighth grade. I can truly say that third grade was an awesome year for me. I learned some of the hardest lessons there was and I passed them all with flying colors.

Chapter 8

4TH GRADE
MRS. LOUISTEEN HARRIS

8 *4th Grade Mrs. Louisteen Harris*

*"And all thy children shall be taught of the Lord,
and great shall be the peace of thy children."*

ISAIAH 54: 13

Fourth grade was the year! It was the class, the teacher, and the grade that every young student longed for. Everybody wanted Mrs. Louisteen Harris for their teacher. I was again laying claim that Mrs. Harris was going to be my favorite teacher and I was going to be the teacher's pet. Mrs. Harris was absolutely beautiful. No ifs, ands, or buts about it. She was about 5 feet 8 inches tall. She had beautiful brown skin. Her hair was always stylish in real cute tight curls. A few curls landed in the center of her forehead.

Mrs. Harris had short, slender fingers. The dimples in her cheeks were so deep they looked as though they were implanted into her jaws. She had a laugh that once you heard it, you could recognize it anywhere. She was just Fun! Fun! Fun! She made learning exciting. The lessons became flesh. Once she taught it, you could eat it. Her lessons became who you were. You walked it, you talked it, and you wanted to sing it. You wanted to impress everybody around you with what you knew so that the upper classmen would ask who is your teacher so you could boldly say, Mrs. Harris. She was like a magnet. You were drawn to her by the smell of her lilac perfume with a hint of honeysuckle, and how she always had time for you. Her dress was absolutely stunning.

Mrs. Harris had this beautiful baby blue and white dress that looked as though someone splashed the two colors together on her dress and each color remained in its right place. She would come out at recess and play tag with us on the poles that held the tin steel roof over our heads to fight the hot rays from the sun so that we could enjoy playing. Mrs. Harris would even jump a few jumps of rope with us. What can I say, Mrs. Harris was just wonderful!

Inside the classroom she challenged us intellectually. We were viewing French films and singing the French songs along with the hand movements to "**Alouette**". In the fourth grade, reading was a big part of her curriculum. She wanted well-rounded readers who could enunciate and pronounce the words correctly. She taught us how to raise our voices when we saw a question mark, and how to pause after the commas, and how to lower our voice when we saw a period and how to show excitement when we saw an exclamation point.

Mrs. Harris invented the reading game of reading until you miss a word. We had red paper-back readers which contained many stories in them. The person who was reading had to read the title, tell who the author was, as well as the illustrator. You also had to stop at all of the end marks and you could not miss a word. Well, you already know that a person would have to go some to beat me reading. When it was my turn to read, you could hear the entire class groan because they knew I was going to read the entire story. One particular day I was reading and Kathryn Ann yelled out I had missed a word. Although I was reading, I stopped long enough to tell on Kathryn. I said, "Kathryn Ann" and Kathryn

Ann yelled out, "Marsha makes me sick" and Mrs. Harris whipped her right then and there. That is not the end of the story - when she was reading, I said the same thing and Mrs. Harris asked the same question, and Kathryn Ann yelled out "Marsha" and I said, "Marsha my foot", and I in turn got a whipping. Amazingly for the most part, we were great friends - we just could not leave the competition alone.

The other side of Mrs. Harris was she was a sensitive person. Sometimes I would ask her if I could stay in with her and I would always help her clean or stack the books - whatever she wanted me to do. I just wanted to be around her. She made me feel good about myself.

Mrs. Harris taught us how to recite our multiplication facts. We were so good we could stand before the class and recite them all by memory. We had the best spelling bee's on this side of Oklahoma - it was called turn me down. You had to out spell the person in the line and then you could keep going. If you ended up the last person in the line you were the best speller. Mrs. Harris' classroom was always neat and orderly. Although we had fun, she still had a control mechanism to her teaching style.

Mrs. Harris was a devoted Christian. She was always at church on her post. She was a great usher. I was so fascinated with her being able to wear many, many hats and I was always proud to tell everybody wherever I went that she was my teacher. No matter how hard things became for us, Mrs. Harris was always there cheering us on, telling us that we could make it and to stay focused.

Mrs. Harris spoke words of wisdom into our lives. She created opportunities for us to be able to display our talents and our abilities. She had a play for the fourth graders to perform and I shall never forget when she selected me to be the main character in the play. I was so happy and I was determined to do my very best. Although my mother could not make it to the play because she had to work, she had me to rehearse my lines to her and she ranted and raved about how good I was. Mother said, "Speak out loud and put your best foot forward. Mamma knows that you are going to do great".

I went to the play all dressed up in my acting clothes. I had memorized my lines and when I looked out and saw my fourth grade teacher, she was laughing harder than anyone. I heard that unique laugh and I heard my mama's voice coaching me on - I knew then that the play was a huge success. As a result of my school experiences on stage, I have no problem speaking in front of crowds today. Although I liked Mrs. Harris, I sometimes would become jealous if she paid attention to any of the other students and she had to tell me, "Marsha, you are too selfish - I have to treat everybody the same". At first I did not understand what she said, so every chance I would get, I would say things about her son like "Old Black Tony Harris makes me sick". Later on after several years, Mrs. Harris would laugh and tease me about how she heard me talking about Tony. She thought that I had a crush on him because he was her son and we had a good laugh about that.

One day I shall never forget - Mrs. Harris allowed me to stay in this particular day from recess. I remember seeing her read a letter and I saw her eyes well up with tears. I did not know why she was crying, but I felt like I wanted to cry with her. I went up to her and asked, "Mrs. Harris why are you crying?", and she replied, my sister just died. She asked me not to mention it to anyone, so when my class mates came back in from recess, Mrs. Harris had dried her eyes and she went on with class as usual. That day I tried my best not to get into any trouble and was on my best behavior because of what I had just learned at recess time. I never revealed her secret to my class -mates, I stayed true to my word. I believe in my heart that this was my first opportunity to exemplify honesty and integrity.

Another memory about Mrs. Harris is that she always told us to go straight home after school and to make sure we did not forget about our younger siblings. She also reminded us not to walk off and leave them and don't forget to do our homework for the night. At school she reminded us that we were not to go on the high school side for any reason and she taught us how we were supposed to act in Chapel. We could not wear pants to school unless it was a cold, rainy, snowy day. If we did wear a pair of pants, we had to wear a dress over them or a skirt. Mrs. Harris wanted us to excel in all our studies. She gave all that she had and she made sure we were prepared for the years to come.

Mrs. Harris' room was the 4th door on the right hand side of the building which made her room the last door on the end. Whenever Mrs. Harris got ready to whip us, she would either borrow Mrs. Rinehart's belt or Miss Boren's strap. Either way, you knew that you were going to be in big time trouble if she went to get the straps because it took a lot to get Mrs. Harris upset. Mrs. Harris was more patient than the other teachers.

One of the things I remember about Mrs. Harris is that she had beautiful handwriting. It was easy to read her letters. They were always formed correctly and they had some flair to them. I excelled in Mrs. Harris' class and by the time school was out, I dreaded leaving her room because she was so much fun, so loving, and so concerned about each of her students. The school year ended on a positive note and once again, we were all promoted to the 5th grade. We all knew what fifth grade meant and we were happy to have been promoted, but realized that a change was going to come. If I had to repeat any grade it would have been my choice to repeat the fourth grade with my favorite teacher Mrs. Louisteen Harris. Every year after I left home I would send Mrs. Harris a birthday card and a dollar bill in it. The memories of her still linger in my heart. When I became a teacher, I was able to teach the fourth grade. So many times I wished she would have been alive to see exactly how much I conducted my classes like she would have. I thank God for the relationship that I had with my favorite teacher, Mrs. Louisteen Harris.

Chapter 9

5TH GRADE
MRS. THELMA RHINEHART

9   *5th Grade Mrs. Thelma Rhinehart*

*"And in the fifth year ye shall eat of the fruit
thereof, that it may yield unto you the increase
thereof. I am the Lord your God."*

LEVITICUS 19:25

Once again we were all promoted to the 5th grade. Our new teacher, Mrs. Thelma Rhinehart, was actually the oldest teacher in the elementary department. She taught all my older siblings, my mother and all her older siblings. I tell you Mrs. Rhinehart had some longevity at Booker T. Washington School. Mrs. Thelma was very renowned. Everybody either knew or heard about her and her black leather strap, which she affectionately called "Dr. Pepper".

Mrs. Rhinehart stood approximately 5 feet, 10 inches tall. She was very bow-legged. She was short-waisted and she kept a stern look on her face at all times. She did not smile very often and her face was splattered with freckles. Mrs. Rhinehart wore her hair back in a simple bun. Her hair was always pulled away from her face. Her fingers were long and slender and were graced by a beautiful wedding set that had square shaped diamonds that extended from one end of the band to the other end.

Mrs. Rhinehart wore dresses that were of steel gray and navy blue. Her lips looked as though they were partially burned on the inside.

Her teeth were evenly shaped from top to bottom. Her nose was pointed from the top and both nostrils were slightly flared at the base of her nose. I can remember during Mrs. Rinehart's instructional history time, she would rub together a particular yellow pencil and every time the center of the pencil would tap against her wedding rings, it would make this clicking sound. All you could hear in Mrs. Thelma's room was the clicking of the pencil against her rings, and her voice.

Mrs. Rhinehart was a stern disciplinarian. When you entered her room, it put you in the mind of a hospital ICU waiting room. The sounds of quietness were embedded in the walls. It rested upon the ceilings and plastered the wall with a quiet stillness. When we were allowed to speak, you spoke almost in a whisper. Mrs. Thelma did not tolerate much. She was a woman of power and control. There was never a question about where your place was. She had a "no nonsense" attitude about everything. She never laughed nor smiled. She meant education all the way. Mrs. Rhinehart whipped you for the least mistake that you made. She was a perfectionist in the worse way.

Everything that you turned into her had to be done a certain way. Every student was expected to make their own spellings pads. The materials consisted of two cardboard pieces cut into strips. At the top of each strip you had to punch holes large enough to put a shoe string in them to hold the papers and the two pieces of card board securely. This project was a must. You had to number your paper one to twenty. You could not write outside the red margins, you could not erase on the paper and you had to be able to spell every word correctly. If you missed a word, she would invite you up to her desk and she would take out her strap, Dr. Pepper, and she would give you a lick in the center of your hand. If you jerked your hand back because of the pain, she would automatically add another lick. This was a sad time in Mrs. Thelma's class because there were some students who really had some challenges with learning and making a 100% was not easy for them to do. I even occasionally missed a word or two.

Every time we had our semester test, Mrs. Thelma would write on the board, "What are the four fundamentals of arithmetic?" of course the answer was addition, subtraction, multiplication, and division, yet many students still missed the question. We had to sit in rows in her class in alphabetical order. We had to write reports and then orally read them to the class as well as be able to recite our math facts and our roman numerals. There was not one easy thing about her class. You learned in her class, but you certainly did not have fun doing it.

At this time we would have school plays combined with Mrs. Louisteen Harris' fourth grade class and this was a happy time for me because I truly did love Mrs. Harris. She would listen intently as the other students would rehearse their lines.

Mrs. Thelma had this clear container with a red top on both ends which resembled a miniature hour glass. On one end it was filled with salt and the other end it was filled with pepper. She would pour some grains of salt in her hands and lick the salt out of her hands in such a dignified way that we did not know what she was doing. Every now and then she would leave it on her desk and that's how we figured out what she was putting in her hands and then into her mouth. She did this periodically as she helped make the decision on which other students would be able to participate in the play. We were all sitting along the window sills and on the floor to make room for Mrs. Harris' students. It was a long process, but finally the next day they gave every one their parts and then the practices would begin.

I was always chosen as the main character in the plays because I had great memory skills. My voice was loud and I did not need a microphone and I was an excellent reader. I really felt great making my teachers proud of my gifts and to be able to help make the plays a success for the school.

At the end of the day on certain days of the week, Mrs. Thelma was given the left-over food from the canteen. She would cut the hot dogs and the greasy sloppy joe's and share them with the students who had money to purchase them. I was not a happy camper in her classroom because it was a time in my life that I truly felt the crunch of mistreatment and rejection. Although I did very well in my studies, I was sad most of the time. Mrs. Thelma would say to me, "Akins, you need to stop frowning. If you don't, there is going to be a permanent indention in your forehead". I really did not know what she meant, but I tried my best not to frown.

By now my mother and father had two more children under me - Debra and Tony. I had no idea she was pregnant again, but I began to feel more and more deprived of everything. The crowning blow was Christmas in my fifth grade year. We all pulled names in Mrs. Thelma's class during the Christmas holiday. We had turkey and dressing, green beans, and mashed potatoes. When I got ready to take my seat, I found a long strand of hair in my dressing. I cried so hard that all of my friends, Booley, Terry, Kathryn Ann, Ruth, and even my cousin Sharon Lue, tried to give me their plate, but I was so hurt and angry at that point that I refused to eat. Mr. Henry Edwards came up and said, "Akins, just take the hair out the food and eat it, you probably are not used to having any food like this anyway". I really cried then because I felt like another shot had been taken at my parents who were doing the very best that they could to provide for us. We might not have had running water, and we had to warm ourselves by a wood stove, and we had to use out-houses, but food and love was one thing we were never lacking. We had plenty of love, food, fun, and each other. I had a big problem with Mr. Edwards for trying to front me in front of all the kids in the cafeteria. I was sad for the rest of the day.

Another incident that was sad to me happened again in 5th grade. Mark Shoals pulled my best friend, Ruth's name to give her a Christmas present. He gave her some pecans, an orange and an apple. Ruth cried so hard I felt sorry for her, but there was nothing that I could do to help except console her as she cried.

I really felt like the straw that broke the camel's back was in February when my mother had another baby. I was so embarrassed because I am a fifth grader and I have a baby sister. I still have three more months before I can become a 6th grader, my sister Bernice was a senior.

In 1965 when Lori Ann was born, mother allowed Bernice to name her. Lori was a pretty baby but I just did not want my classmates to know that I had another sibling. This particular morning mother dropped me off at school in front of Mrs. Thelma's classroom and all my friends came running to the car to speak to Mrs. Bobbie. Kathryn Ann was leading the pack. When she saw Lori laying in the seat she begged mother to let her hold her and she did. Kathryn Ann began to show Lori off to everybody. I was so mad I felt like I could have strangled her. I survived that hurdle and Kathy kept saying, "Marsha you should be ashamed of yourself".

I really did love my siblings; it's just that we were so poor I was wondering would I ever be able to get anything except the same black doll with curls over her head in a cute pink pleated dress. Kenneth was going to use her head that could be screwed off for a ball. Well, I made it through the fifth grade with flying colors. We were all promoted to the 6th grade but this time it was different. Mrs. Thelma made everything suspenseful. You really did not know if you were going to be promoted or demoted. Good news once again - we were all promoted. The year was a long, hard struggle, but we still remained loyal to each other. We had started out together since first grade and now we were becoming more and more like family. After all, we were now sixth graders.

Chapter 10

6TH GRADE
MR. HERMAN STEWART

10   *6th Grade Mr. Herman Stewart*

"There are six things that the Lord hates. Haughty eyes, lying tongue, hands that shed innocent blood, a heart that devises wicked plans, feet that run rapidly to evil, a false witness who utter lies, and one who spreads strife among brothers."

PROVERBS 6:17

Kathryn and I became very close during our 3rd, 4th, 5th and 6th grade years. We had just completed our 5th grade year and it was summer. Kathryn Ann started asking my mother if I could spend the night with her. Of course mother said yes and we had some of the best fun times.

Kathryn was the only girl in her family, but her cousin Odell was living with her and they were like brother and sister. Odell was always a lot of fun although he was much older than we were. He used to love for me to come over because it seemed like it was always his time to wash dishes and I was taught when you spend the night away from home, always help out wherever you were needed. So Odell was glad when I came over because I would wash the dishes for him.

These rules included: make your bed as soon as you get out of it, thank the people for the food, say your grace, clean the kitchen up after each meal, stay out of the way of grown folk and their conversation, and learn how to say "No thank you".

All my life I wanted a pair of galoshes and a raincoat, but the closest I ever came to owning these things was when Kathryn Ann wore hers. She had the works, red galoshes, a raincoat, gloves plus a ride home in bad weather.

We had to walk all the way to the *Belmont Addition* in the rain, the sleet, the snow and the sunshine. We couldn't ride with our neighbors because most of the time they had to make room in their cars for everyone in their family and they outnumbered us. In spite of all this, we accepted the fact that our parents had work to do and could not take off because of the weather. God blessed us and we were still honor students. The Lord blessed again and our parents were able to purchase a brand new Jim Walter home on 1201 East Medlock Street in the *Belmont Addition*.

Come with me as I change the tense of this part of the book so that you can experience what I experienced as I lived in our new home.

"We have an apple orchard in the yard and hardwood floors." My brother Charlie keeps the floors waxed and shined. We have three bedrooms, and a bathroom, (no more outhouses!). We have a living room that is beautiful, but more than anything, we have doors!! No more quilts and bedspreads to cover up the missing doors. Life is great. We have our first telephone with the number FA6-3175 and we still have the same phone number to this day.

We play all summer and our chores have changed because now we can wash the dishes in a sink instead of in two dish pans. One of the pans was for washing the dishes, and the other pan was for rinsing the dishes. We have a utility room with a washer and dryer instead of an old-fashioned ringer washer and a rinse tub. We no longer have to take baths in a number 3 tin tub. Life is so great now!"

"I am 10 years old and we are living in a brand new home, one of the first in the **Belmont Addition.** School is starting again and I have almost lost my thrill for it. Time and things are changing and it is rumored that we are going to have to go to the white school after this year.

Our 6th grade teacher is going to be Mr. Herman Stewart. He is a big tall man with a thick black mustache. His hair is cut real low to his head and it is rumored that he is super mean, that he walks softly and carries a big stick. His paddle is called "The Board of Education". Mr. Stewart could play the saxophone and sing like none other to us. He always had an air of confidence about him no matter what he was doing. He was a prancing man when he would move in your presence. It was always with a prance and a stance that suggested that he was a music man.

We finally entered into our sixth year. This is the first year that we have different teachers for each class. Mr. Stewart calls the roll and yes, I am still the first one to be called, but even this is losing its allure. He is quite different in his teaching style. For instance, he has us to go to a map on the board and he calls out the name of a country and we have to find it. I remember it was my turn to go and I pronounced the name of the country called Czechoslovakia. He gave me a raving review for pronouncing the name correctly.

This was good for my low self-esteem. I guess I was growing up because I was more interested in what was going on with the older schoolmates.

Being still young, we were forbidden to go over to the other side of the school. I felt tempted like Eve when she tasted the apple. I had to know what was going on over on that side. I, being an instigator, called my classmates together and asked them if they were willing to go over to the high school side with me and everyone agreed. I led the way and everyone else ran behind me. We were running in the hallways ducking and dodging and looking for Mr. Stewart. We saw all kinds of fun things going on.

Our greatest nightmare happened - we ran right smack dab into Mr. Stewart. Mr. Stewart had his arms folded and we bumped right into him. We took off in the other direction. The school bell rang and all the other students were in their classrooms but us. It seems as though it took Mr. Stewart forever to come back and give out our punishments. Everybody started accusing me and the kids all started crying. Being Miss Tough Girl, I was not going to let them see me cry. If I got a whipping then so be it.

When Mr. Stewart came back into the room, he asked how we would like to get our whipping and Larry Westfield spoke up and said "Ladies are always trying to be first, then let the Ladies be first". This is the one time when I wished the alphabet started with another letter because Mr. Stewart decided to go in alphabetical order. I was so angry I kicked the trash can over. All you could hear was a lot of crying going on, but nevertheless, we survived.

Mr. Stewart was the only male teacher that we had at Booker T. so the change was quite different. It wasn't that he was any meaner than the female teachers; it was his mere height, strength, and his voice that could be intimidating. While we were in Mr. Stewart's class, we had pull out or should I say, we had enrichment programs. I remember having to go to Mrs. Lottie Thompson's class. She was about 6 feet tall and slender. She had gray hair and she wore wide-framed eye glasses. She spoke barely above a whisper, and you know that drove me out of my mind!

We had to read from a screen with a projector. It had black film that you had to place into the mouth of the projector. After each sentence, you could hear this clicking sound to indicate that the next sentence was coming up. I absolutely hated it because I could read. Why did I have to go through this boring reading film? One day I started talking and Mrs. Thompson put me out of her class. I stood outside the door so long that I began counting the bricks on the wall of the classroom.

The recess bell rang and I went to play with my friends and when recess was over, my friends told me that Mrs. Thompson said that I could come back into the classroom. Well you know me; I went strutting back into her classroom. She looked up and recognized that I was in her class. In her quiet voice, she politely asked me what I was doing in her class. I told her my classmates said that she sent for me to come back in. She told me to go right back outside, and of course, another big laugh on Marsha.

The other pull out that we had was a math class. We had to go to Mrs. Adams' class for math. I really hated math and Mrs. Adams talked really low as well. She was the principal's wife. She wore wire-framed glasses and her hair was always disheveled. She had a gap in the front of her teeth. She used a red pencil that marked our bad behaviors. Every time she caught you laughing or talking, you would get a red mark.

One day Ruth and I were talking and Mrs. Adams asked us to stop. When we didn't stop, she gave us 3 red marks and politely took out her strap and asked Ruth and me to come up front. Ruth in her slow monotone voice asked, "Mrs. Adams can we go to the basement?" and Mrs. Adams mocked Ruth and replied in the same tone, "You weren't talking in the basement". This made everybody in class laugh. They laughed so hard it took Mrs. Adams a while to calm the class down. So here we go again - another whipping.

We were told at the end of the school year that segregation was over and our school would be closed. We were going to be attending Benjamin Franklin School. That summer was definitely different and we knew we were in for a change. Precious memories, how they linger.

Chapter 11

JR. HIGH DAYS

11   *Jr. High Days*

Here we go again - another set back. We had to leave our wonderful school, Booker T. and attend Benjamin Franklin Jr. High School because of integration. I had a big problem dealing with integration and being separated from all of my classmates. We were in a new school, new principal, new teachers, new environment and a whole new way of learning.

Our roots where we got started from were being pulled up from under us, our play ground, our gymnasiums, our swings and slides, the jump ropes, the jacks - everything that caused us to become a close knit family was now being shred into pieces. Our new principal at the school was Mr. Walter Leonard. He was a tall Caucasian male. You could tell instantly that he did not want us at the school anymore than we wanted to be there.

Benjamin Franklin Jr. High had an upstairs and downstairs. It had lockers with combinations that I hated. Ruth and I were locker mates. Our locker was right next to a boy named Mike Nathan. He was a good looking boy to me. He had olive skin. He wore his hair in a beetle haircut and I remember teasing him. I took his keys and hid them and he told on me. My first week of school, and I was already in trouble.

We had to change classes, find the location of the room, and remember our locker combinations. Of course I was always late. I hated going to science class upstairs. The teacher was Mr. Hilburn. He had a son in our grade that looked just like him. Everything was just different. I yelled the answers out if I knew them; I talked if I did not know the answer. One day I was sent to the principal's office. I went straight to the office, picked the telephone up and called mother to come and get me. He made me hang the phone up. I thought, "I can't win for loosing".

Kathryn Ann and Mae Etta became good friends and Glenda Faye and I started hanging with them at lunch. Every day we would walk to lunch together and Mae Etta and Kathryn Ann were already smoking cigarettes and they asked me and Glenda if we wanted to learn how to smoke. You know I was game, so Mae Etta took a nice long drag and swallowed the smoke and blew it out of her mouth and her nostrils. Kathryn Ann did the same thing, and then Glenda tried it and it worked. Just as soon as I got ready to take my turn, I heard this old familiar voice ringing from out of nowhere saying, "You better drop it!"

I knew it was my Aunt Juanita, but I could not see her. I dropped it and ran. I hated to go home because I knew the news had already beaten me there. I found out later that she was working at the Webb Hotel and she had taken a break and was looking out of the window on about the fourth floor and she could not only see, she could hear what the kids were saying. Needless to say, after that I never desired to learn how to smoke.

I had many lessons from our friends who were very much more mature than I was. The saddest part of the commentary was

Kathryn Ann and her family moved to Bakersfield, California and Glenda and her family moved to Phoenix, Arizona.

The next year, school was not fun. I felt like I was living in Alaska. One day after school I was walking home, doing my usual, making everybody laugh and I noticed this little girl who was cute as a button. She had long beautiful hair, very petite and she laughed at everything I said. I asked her what her name was and she said Sharon Gage. She invited me to go home with her, and I did.

When I arrived at her house, I saw this real good looking guy bouncing a basketball off the roof of the house. He had on some burnt orange slacks and a white shirt. I asked who was he, and Sharon answered nonchalantly, "Oh, that's just my brother Gary Joe". Little did I know that he would be the guy who would change my whole life in a matter of minutes. As time went on, school was even more of a disappointment for me.

Nothing worked well for me in middle school. I just wanted it all to end so that I could move on to the next year to see if things were going to be different. That summer, Sharon and I spent a lot of time together. We became very close. She could always make me laugh and I always made her laugh.

I remember Marva Jo, who bore the same middle name as me. Marva, Sharon and I had great fun together. Marva was just as funny as I thought I was. I remember when Marvin Gay had this hit out - "What's Going on?" Marva declared that his first words to that song were "Marva, Marva". We went over to listen closely and every time he would say it, I kept telling her that wasn't what he was saying and she would start the 45 record all over again. We never agreed that that was what he was saying, so we just agreed to disagree. It was still so much fun.

We used to walk up and down the street and just laugh out loud at what we were saying to each other. Everybody would say, "That is Marsha Jo". Yes, I have always had a loud voice, so I enjoyed it. Sharon and I did many exciting things together. Although Gary was her brother, it never interfered with our relationship. We just enjoyed sharing our secrets, laughing and enjoying each other's company.

Sharon was very pretty and equally as smart. She was her mother's only daughter and she learned all the domestic things. She could cook and sew. That wasn't very interesting to me because daddy was not going to eat anybody's cooking except my mother's, so I concentrated on learning how to clean, wash, and iron.

In spite of all the fun we had, it was now time to get ready for the upcoming school year. Once again, another change in my life, we now have to go back to Booker T. Washington for the 9th grade. I thought, "What could be more devastating than to have to go back to a place you were taken from in the 6th grade, only to return three years later". It made no sense at all to me, but I went with the flow and started my 9th grade year at Booker T. Washington, the home of the Hornets.

Chapter 12

REJECTION

12 *Rejection*

I have just completed my eight year of school, and isn't it ironic that the educational system sends us back to Booker T. Washington, (The all Black School), to take classes. You talking about tossing and turning, shifting, and moving, that's where we were.

Mae Etta had had her baby when she came back to enroll to go to the 9th grade with us. She was as pretty as ever. She wore her hair in the cutest styles. She was small and petite. She was very sharp when it came to the things of life. As I said earlier, we were a very close knit group of children and we were always accepting of each other. I remember Mae Etta coming two days to class with us and we had a ball catching up on all the things we had missed since we had last seen each other. Kathryn Ann and Glenda Faye had already moved to the west coast. Mae had a pretty little girl and now she was going to come back to school with us.

We were in Mrs. Terrell's Home Economics class. She was one of those teachers who did everything in a prim and proper fashion. She had a whiny kind of voice. She wore her bluish gray hair pulled back in a bun with a few bangs in the front. She had wire-framed eyeglasses that rested upon her nose most of the time. She wanted us to have class and become well rounded in all areas of life.

All of us were so poor we could not appreciate the worth of knowing that there was a difference between marmalade and jelly, butter and margarine. Who cared? We just wanted the rolls to be cooked so that we could put the sweet spread, the jelly-like substance that she called marmalade, on the bread and eat them until they were all gone.

Mrs. Terrell was concerned about educating us. Did I care about how to sit at a table when all of our plates at home did not match anyway. What difference did it make that a fork and a knife or a spoon each had a place at the table when most of the times we did not have enough silverware to go around, some foods were eaten with our fingers anyway. Who cares about glasses? We broke up the ones mother had and had to drink out of tin or plastic cups anyway.

At that point in my life I was intrigued with going into the beautiful sitting room with the beautiful couches and chair, and coffee tables and lamps. Just to get away with Mae Etta, Ruth, Berlinda, and Sharon Lou so we could just take in all the wonderful things that Mae Etta knew.

Another disappointment came that second day of school. Mae Etta was called to the office at the end of the day. After she left the office, she came to tell us that she had bad news. She could no longer go to school with us because she had had a baby out of wedlock and she was not married. Something on the inside of me rose up. I was so hurt and disappointed, again. I wanted to cry for her. I just did not know what to do with what I was feeling on the inside.

In spite of all that, I had an extremely great year. I was smart, very popular, had many friends, was very competitive, and popular. I was the freshman basketball queen and James Terry Fort (Booley) was the captain of the team and he escorted me across the floor. My name was up in spotlights - boy - those were the days. You know, as I look back over my life, I think about how every time God would bless me, the devil would always come in and start a mess.

Helen Babb was a very pretty girl and she could sing like a bird. Helen, however, wanted to be the Basketball queen, so she took my crown before the game and hid it. Little did Helen and I know that this would be the last time that I would ever be able to participate in another school function.

I finally made it to the end of the year. I shall never forget the prophecy that Mrs. Terrell spoke over my life at the end of the school year. She said to me, "Akins, you aren't going to make it far". This was my first encounter with the spirit of **rejection**, whose purpose was to eject me out of my God-given position. Little did I know that the next year I would be another statistic like my friend, Mae Etta.

Chapter 13

WHAT HAPPENED, I'M PREGNANT

13   *What Happened? I'm Pregnant!*

How could this be? I did not really know what the word pregnant meant. And yet I am what I do not know.

I remember calling my friend Kathryn Ann all the way in California and asking her, "Can you get pregnant by kissing?" I never had a menstrual period until I was 15 years of age, and now I try this thing that they call love. I discovered that love is a far cry from having sex with someone who you think you are so in love with.

I shall never forget coming home after school was out. I was so sleepy that I could not stay awake. I had chores around the house to complete, I had my homework to finish, but I absolutely could not muster up enough energy to get anything done. I remember sleeping so long that I could not get up in enough time to perform my daily duties. Since I had missed the summer season of my life, I had to shift gears and deal with the one that I was in at this time.

I wanted to become a little girl all over again. I wanted to do everything I use to do I wanted to do anything that I thought would turn back the hands of time for me. I wanted to jump rope again. I wanted to play jacks. I wanted to play "this is the way you villa volley". I wanted to play "Mary Mack all dressed in black", but I was only fooling myself. It was over - never to be again, so I took it like a good solider. I could not cry, I could not even express what I felt inside. I knew I was so embarrassed and hurt. I was in a place called "torment", so I lived there praying and believing that I could make it through another day.

I remember being big as a horse and everybody was getting ready for the prom and it dawned on me another chapter in my life that no one would ever be able to read. I never got the opportunity to go, but I made it through all of that. Shirley Bostic, who was Gary's first cousin, was a few years older than I. She was pregnant as well. She and I lived a few houses from each other so we became very close. We did a lot of sharing with each other. Her mother whom I called Aunt Gloria Helen, had a charge account with Holton's grocery store, and Carol, Shirley's oldest sister, would come by and give us a ride to the store and we would buy those Vienna cookies and bologna and strawberry soda. Those were the days. At least when I was with Carol and Shirley, I could always laugh and enjoy their company. Carol was always telling us about the Lord.

It was the night time that I hated because I asked myself a million times why and I could never get the answer so I would fall asleep believing that maybe tomorrow this nightmare would come to a screeching halt but it never did.

Instead of counting my mistake, I began counting my months until it was time that I would deliver. I remember my sister Jewel was such a jewel. She did everything in her power to make me happy. She told me big sister secrets of how to care for my baby. She went with me to pick out the things that I would need and because she had so many children, she kept me abreast about the labor and delivery and yes, I was even more frightened, but I knew that she would be with me if no one else showed up.

Jewel came and spent time with me every day. We would laugh and ride and talk about the funny remarks Mama Mag would say. I remember all too well Mama Mag said to me one day, "Marsha you are going to have a boy". I don't know how old folks could look at you and tell you things that actually came true. So I started looking forward to the day that I would deliver. It finally came to me to believe it - you are pregnant and soon you will enter into the world called motherhood. At that point "What Happened, I Am Pregnant" really was not a question any longer it was now a statement. Yes, at 15 years of age, I was pregnant.

Chapter 14

HE LOVES ME, HE LOVES ME NOT

14   *He Loves Me, He Loves Me Not*

My life has been one of long struggles, many valleys and every now and then some peaks, and yes even some mountain top experiences. As I look back over my life, I must admit that I have not regretted one minute of it. I have made some foolish mistakes and some wise choices. I have desired to be loved, and have been rejected. I have been accepted and at other times, I have been abandoned. I have been lonely, and yet I have been in a place called alone.

There have been times I have wounded others, and in turn have been broken in the inward parts. I have held grudges, and have seen through the eyes of a tunnel vision. But today I have asked for forgiveness and have forgiven those who have hurt, despised, mistreated, misused and talked about me even when I came to a point in my life when I did not know which way to go. When I was not sure which path I should embark upon, something on the inside of me gave me the courage and the strength to keep going in the direction that I was headed. This inward voice would also caution me when I needed to mark time and wait. I later discovered that this voice that I often heard was the voice of the Holy Spirit.

I felt like my life was staring down a double-barreled bazooka with some one playing Russian roulette with my emotions. How can you go from being happy, believing that you are in love, and then be sadly oppressed because what you thought was love was nothing more than getting in the way of a semi-diesel to have your feelings crushed right before your very eyes. How could I have lost everything in one deal? Was I that bad of a bargainer? Did I really think that I was old enough to believe that I knew what love was? What is this thing called love? My mother told me as a little girl that love was a green-eyed monster, but Gary Joe Gage did not resemble a green-eyed monster to me at all. In fact, he was good-looking; he had a smile that took a minute before it would reach the other end of his mouth; his eyebrows were short dark and distinct.

Gary's mustache covered his top lip perfectly. His eyes were absolutely beautiful. They looked as though they were dancing in their sockets because he could look at you and look away as quickly as he looked at you the first time. He had a quiet demeanor. He was not loud or boisterous. Because he was so mysteriously quiet, it made him that much more attractive. This was the year that the scales were removed from my eyes. I was the middle child in my family and now I realized that all my life I suffered with MCS & LSE - yes - Middle Child Syndrome and Low Self-Esteem. Anybody will tell you that's like taking a drink of whiskey and chasing it with narcotics. It is too much for the mind to contain.

I was so thrilled to be going into the 10th grade with all my friends and to be emerged into the school system with all the children who went to school with me at Booker T. Boy, life was great and I really thought that I had it going on because I thought that Gary Gage was my boyfriend. Little did I know that Gary Gage had another girlfriend. I was so mesmerized by the fact that he was so good-looking and fun. He would show up at unexpected times and then just as quickly as he showed up, he would be gone.

I remember the pep rallies we use to have downtown on Broadway to cheer the football team on for the upcoming games. It was just fun to be in the crowd where the atmosphere was that of laughter, talking, yelling and screaming. This was a side of school that I had never experienced.

By now I had come out of the eighth and ninth grade stupor, after all, I was a big sophomore. I distinctly remember Gary walking me home for the first time. It was Gary, my brother Kenneth, and me. Gary carried my books and I thought I was in heaven. All this individualized attention on me was more than I could imagine. Wow! He had on this white trench coat and it was double breasted and he left the top buttons hanging loose and he did not fasten the belt into the buckle - the belt just hung down at his side. We laughed and talked all the way to the *Belmont Addition*. It was cold, so we took the trail that we had made by walking the path the same way everyday. It was what we called the short cut.

I immediately took him down to my sister, Ruby Jewel's house. I think she liked him a lot because if Jewel did not approve of you, you would be able to tell by the way she acted. He went over to where my nephews Anthony and Vincent were shooting marbles. Gary asked them what they were playing and they could not say the name of the game – "Flucks". He continued to ask them and he would laugh over and over again. How foolish of me to think walking me home, laughing with my nephews and meeting my sister Jewel, would be all that it would take. Wrong again.

Now that I look back, Gary and I would talk a lot on the telephone, but we really did not do anything public. However because my best friend was his sister, Sharon, I saw him a lot more than normal. She would always write on his mirror if he was not at home when I called to make sure he would call me. I became terribly obsessed with him. He became the air that I inhaled, he was my every thought. By now I realized that he was talking to another girl and the desire to get him became more and more addictive. I did not care what it took at that moment, and finally I made a decision that I thought would make me happy for the rest of my life, but ultimately the consequences were worse than the sin that I had committed.

I lost. I lost everything in a matter of 15 minutes. I lost my virginity, my self-worth, my self-esteem, my freedom, my friends, and the most important thing, I lost him. When I came to my senses, I felt like the prodigal daughter who had waddled in the hog pen of pity, shame, insecurity, and defeat. I was awakened the next morning by Mr. Sun shining down on me, not because it was a beautiful day, but to remind me of what I had done that was a sin and a shame.

The wind reminded me that what I had done was a terrible detestable thing. Almost immediately, my body did a metamorphic twist and I knew something was wrong, but I had no idea that I was pregnant. The first sign was I could not stop sleeping. I could not get my chores done and I did not have time to study properly. I could not take it anymore. At night I could not sleep. The light from the moon would remind me that I was in trouble and that I had no one to turn to. I had no friends that would keep my secret, but I knew that I had better tell my mother what was going on, but I could not tell her. Then it became too much for me to handle.

Gary had completely stopped talking to me. What did I do wrong? I thought he told me that he loved me and that we were going to be together. What did I get myself into? How was I going to get out of this knot that I had allowed myself to get into. Finally I went to my mother and I told her who I was pregnant by; and that he had another girl pregnant as well. Mrs. Dorothy Bradley had already told her who she had heard the father was. My mother was quite calm. She was determined not to involve Gary's parents in having to be financially responsible for having to help take care of the baby.

That day reality set into every fiber of my being. The news flashes of "If I could just go to school" well, that was over. No more school no more friends, no more laughter. No more honey-honey be bop, no more going to the town fair, no more talking on the telephone, no Junior-Senior prom, no more football, basketball games and you got it, no more boyfriend because by now, Gary had somebody else pregnant and they were on with their lives.

I felt like I was at the lowest of the lowest. All I had was my big sister Jewel. Here I am in the first quarter of my sophomore year when I should have been enjoying all the activities that came with school. Instead, the Hugo High School administrators said, "You must go home. You cannot attend this school anymore because you are pregnant and you are not married".

Mr. Parker, the school superintendent, with those wide-brim black eyeglasses, had the sternest look on his face. I slowly turned around clothed with the jacket of embarrassment, the collar of hurt, and the buttons of rejection. As I walked down the stairs on my way home, I had no one to talk to, no where to go, and nothing to do except wait eight months to deliver. I am sure my mother was more hurt than I. My father was more discouraged than both of us.

My siblings were in a place of bewilderment which changed the course of our lives forever. My mother was a strong devout woman of God. She knew how to pray and she lived the life she talked about. She knew how to handle adverse situations. Everyday of our lives, my mother instilled the things of God into us. She quoted scriptures with wisdom to get us in order. When we wanted to go play with our friends or cousins more than we should, she would say, "Go get the Bible". She would then make you turn to the scripture that said "withdraw your foot from your neighbor's house lest he will become weary of you and hate you".

When we would act wild and rowdy and act as though we had no home training, she would say "stop acting like those uncircumcised Philistines" or she would say "you all are going to make me loose my religion". Sometime she would say "treat others the way you want to be treated". Or she would say "you are going to reap what you sow" and on and on and on.

But at this point I think she became angry with the devil. My oldest brother Arbrey, was in Viet Nam, my sister Jewel had just lost her husband in the Viet Nam war. Times were hard. Charley had three girls pregnant at the same time, and he had not graduated from High school. And now her daughter at the age of 15 is pregnant. The system will not allow her to go to school and yet they allowed Gary, the father, to continue his education. I think her righteous indignation rose up, even more.

Mother's love for her helpless child superseded all her ability to think straight. She and I went down to Mr. and Mrs. Gage's house to talk to Gary and his family. Mother did not want them to have to be responsible for the baby, but she did say these words to Gary, "Gary since they will not let Marsha go to school and they will not stop you. Let's help give her a chance", she said "if you will marry her, you don't have to take care of her, she don't have to spend a night with you, allow her the opportunity to finish school so that she can take care of her baby", she said "I will personally annul the marriage".

He looked at my mother in front of both his parents and said, "Mrs. Bobbie, I am not ready to get married". Mother told him "Thank you and that she understood". We left, and my mother never said another word about it.

Mother told me "This is what you are going to do. And once again she repeated the same words over to me again. You are going to take care of yourself so that you can deliver a healthy baby". She said "I am going to grow your little girl's mind up to your grown woman's body". She said "leave him alone, he does not want you or any part of the baby. Just know this is your baby and you are going to have to love and take care of the baby regardless". She said the friends that you have; I want you to stay away from them. I am going to tell you as your mother in love, so that you won't get your feelings hurt when their mothers tell them to stay away from you. As far as church goes, you will not flaunt yourself around the saints of God. You can stay home until you can come back to the church, go in front of the church and get it straight". She said "Ask God to forgive you and forgive yourself". Everything was happening so quickly that I felt like I was on the potter's wheel being turned, pulled, and twisted until I became dizzy.

My sister Jewel felt sorry for me. She came every day to give me a ride to Cowlings Grocery store just so I could see Gary as he drove the school bus filled with my classmates back over to Booker T for lunch. At that point in my life, one look was enough for me. I never lost hope. I believed that as time would go on, Gary would have a change of heart and he would come back marry me and we would raise our child together. Again I was wrong - he loves me not.

Chapter 15

THE BOUNCING BABY BOY

15   *The Bouncing Baby Boy!*

I shall always remember September 17, 1971. This was the day that would change the course of my life. The greatest happening in the history of Hugo, Oklahoma, was the opening of their new theater. The theater was right in the heart of the city on the main street called Jackson Street. The movie that came to town was called "Shaft" starring Richard Roundtree.

Everybody and their mama went to see the movie, except me. Guess where I was? You got that right - I was at home ready to deliver my baby. It started earlier that day. I was craving cabbage, cornbread, and fish. C.V. - Gary's dad brought me the fish and I was preparing the cornbread and the cabbage. I could not wait to eat - it smelled so good. Within a matter of a few minutes, I did something that I had not done the entire 9 months that I was pregnant – I threw up. So there went that meal I wanted so desperately.

Immediately after that episode, I started experiencing labor pains. I had never felt this type of pain before. The pains started about 10:00 a.m. and mother started timing the pains. They would stop and start all day. I was in so much pain. Around 7:00 p.m., the pains started coming more fiercely and closer. I wasn't crying, screaming, or yelling, but anyone could tell that the pain was getting unbearable. By this time, daddy had come home. He became nervous and said, "Bobbie, get the girl to the hospital - stop slowing around".

Mother and my sister, Jewel, took me over to the Choctaw County Memorial Hospital where I was ushered off to what they called the Labor Room. It was the dullest, coldest, room I had ever seen. There was nothing on the wall but a clock and nothing in the room but a bed. My sister Jewel had on a yellow and white plaid dress and she stayed right in the room with me. She and my mother were both waiting with quiet faces and never saying a word. They just continued to count the minutes silently until it was time for me to deliver.

The pain became more and more intense. I don't know if I was too afraid to cry or if the pain was so bad that I thought if I made a sound that it would hurt more than what it was already, so I just kept silent. All of a sudden I felt the worse pain I had ever witnessed in my life. The only way I could describe it at 16 years old was, imagine having to urinate really bad for two days and you can't, and somebody taking the Empire State building and placing it on top of your bladder and you still can't urinate. In my mind, that's what it felt like.

All I could remember was the old wives tale that the death angel passes around your bed 7 times while you are in labor and that you could die giving birth. So my labor was not only painful, it was tormenting as well. I remember not wanting to die at 16 and I asked God to forgive me and the next thing that I remembered was being wheeled to the delivery room and the nurses lifted me off the bed and put me onto another bed and I saw this tank at my head that looked liked an oxygen tank and someone slapping this metal black cup over my mouth and nose. I could smell something and I heard this whispering sound. The odor I smelled was like gas and the only thing I remembered seeing was my doctor's wide black eyeglasses. At that point, my eyelids gave away to sleep.

When I awakened, I remember the doctor placing my baby on my stomach. Dr. Lacroix said that after 12 hours of labor, I was a great patient. I had a healthy boy who weighed 8 pounds and 7 ounces and he was 22 inches long. I don't know what emotion I felt at the time. All I knew was that I was so very glad that part of my life was over. I was put into a regular room and My Aunt Willie Mae had got up out of the bed to come and see us. I remember her coming in saying that he was a fine boy and I remember gasping as though I had to go through labor again. She said that part is all behind you, now go to sleep. Starting tomorrow your work will be cut out for you for the rest of your life.

I remember mother, Jewel, and Aunt Willie Mae leaving at midnight that night. I went to sleep and the next morning as soon as visiting hours were started, my room was packed all day and all night. Everyone was coming to see the bouncing baby boy. Mother had this cute little blue book with names in it and she told me that I was not going to name the baby Gary and to start looking for another name.

I guess she knew what I had in mind - so we selected a name together – Kerwin. My best childhood friend, Ruth, named him Dawand. She had two nephews who had been named Dawand and since they still considered me as their family, wanted him to carry their family name also. Mother, Ruth and I named him Kerwin Dawand.

When the certificate was brought for me to sign, it read:

Certificate of Live Birth

State File Number 135

Kerwin Dawand Akins

September 17, 1971

Time: 10:36 P.M.

Male, single birth

County of Birth: Choctaw

City and Town: Hugo

Hospital: Choctaw Memorial

Mother's Name: Marsha Jo Akins   Age: 16

Street Address: 1201 East Medlock and a place for my signature.

My writing looked like a frightened little girl and the place for the father to sign was left blank. It read, "Father Unknown". I felt terrible because that was not a true statement. I knew all too well who the father was, but his father refused to sign the birth certificate. He did not want to own Kerwin as being his child which would include assuming the responsibility of providing for him. The one good thing I can say is that he came to the hospital the next morning, which was Saturday September 18, 1971 to see Kerwin. Gary had on a pair of slacks that were green intermingled with black paisley-like corduroy. He also had on a black shirt to match his pants and a pair of black shoes. It seemed like I had not seen him in ages. He spoke and spent most of his time looking at Kerwin in the Nursery window.

I remember my brother Charlie was there and he asked Gary what was his son's name. Gary tried to pronounce his name but it sounded like "Karin" and everybody started laughing. Well, I did not see Gary anymore while I was in the hospital. I was still happy that he came to see Kerwin. I was still thinking in my mind that he would at least be kind to Kerwin even though he did not want me to be a part of his life. Well, every good thought that I thought was so off base. The truth of the matter was - it was over.

Gary's brother, Travis, had gone to Viet Nam at the same time that my brother Arbrey went. They were both released from the service and Travis had purchased a black and white Malibu. It was a beautiful car. He allowed Gary to drive it a lot, but he never came to the **Belmont** to see Kerwin, although he did bring his mother one time. She and Sharon came to see Kerwin and they brought Pampers, formula and baby clothes, but nothing from Gary. After facing these hard facts, I went on with my life and did what I could do - and that was - not go to school and stay home and take care of my son. I really tried to make the best out of a bad situation.

When I went home from the hospital, mother gave me my first lessons. She said:

"Rule number 1 - You will not spoil him. Your dad and I have to go to work and your siblings have to go to school

Rule number 2 - You will buy cloth diapers and you will wash them daily and hang them on the line we cannot afford pampers.

Rule number 3 - At night when he cries, you will get up pour his formula in the pot, and heat it up. Take the baby with you - put him across your lap, shake him gently until the milk is ready. If the milk is too hot, you have to run cold water over it to cool it down. In the meantime, the inside of your wrist is the thermometer. If it burns you, it is too hot for him

Rule number 4 - You will get up in the morning make sure he is bathed, fed, full and lay him on the bed. The bed can hold him better than you and longer than you. Hold him while you are feeding him so that he can feel loved, then allow him to rest peacefully on the bed.

Rule number 5 - I will not baby-sit for you. You have nothing to do but take care of your baby. This is what you wanted, so here it is."

I took my whipping well. I did exactly what my mother told me to do and I became attached to my baby. I became over protective and I would not let anyone hold him. I did not ask anyone to babysit him. Yet I longed to go to school.

I sat home in that house on Medlock Street in the *Belmont Addition* and I almost lost my mind. I still had not cried, I still had not heard from Gary. The only thing that changed so desperately in my life was that Gary never accepted me or his son Kerwin. He never did anything for his birthday or Christmas. He joined the U.S. Army, married the other girl and end of story, he loved me not.

Then one day out of the blue, God sent another ray of hope to let me know that he had not forgotten about me. Once again my hope was rekindled – yes, even with the Bouncing Baby Boy.

Chapter 16

GUILTY AS CHARGED

16 *Guilty As Charged*

Judge not that you be not judged for with the same judgment you judge you will be judged, and with the measure you use, it will be measured back.

MATTHEW 7:1-3

The hour is starring me in the face. Time has run out. I now have to deal with myself about myself. How can I do this when I don't know who I really am. I know I have crossed over the separation line. I am not a woman, yet my body has all the evidence that I am. My mind is still trapped in a little girl state. I really do not know if I am going or coming or if I am coming and going at the same time.

I hear the sound of youth in the wind. There is a fresh smell of happiness in the air. My friends are all enjoying the spring time of their life and I am in my winter season without a coat. When does it all end? I had just come through the worst storm I have ever known on September 17, 1971. The storm was so fierce I did not hear the wind blowing, I did not smell the rain coming, and I did not hear the sound of thunder. I was so blindly in love I did not even see the lightning flashing. Boy what a storm!

It is almost Christmas time - thank God Kerwin is too young to know about gifts at Christmas time because he will only be 3 months old. All mother and daddy could do was to help buy his milk. I could forget Christmas for myself. What a sad Christmas at 16 years old - no gifts, no friends, no relationship, no contact with Gary. It was a sure thing that he wasn't going to buy Kerwin anything. But one thing was certain, we would have a wonderful dinner and my family would all be home and we had a strong love between us. Just the thought of that brightened my spirits for the time being.

Loneliness had become my best friend, and hurt was my closest enemy. Oppression weighed me down daily, and disappointment was my new conscience. No matter how hard I tried to medicate myself, the medicine of trying to convince myself that Gary was going to have a change of heart, and that one day it would all be better for Kerwin and me, the more disillusioned I became. Every time I tried to cover the wound of my past, the band aid continued to fall off and as soon as disappointment reminded me of what I had done, the wound would start to bleed and the pain would start all over again.

At that point in my life I truly felt like I was in jail waiting on my prison sentence. The word is out - *news flash* - Marsha Akins had a baby by Gary Gage and she cannot go back to school unless she gets married. From all observations, it is apparent that he is not interested in her or her baby. I thought life has got to be better than this. What can I do? Where can I go? Who will just listen and let me talk? I felt like I was losing my mind. I refused to shed a tear even after 12 hours of hard labor the tears would not come. Yet there was a part of me that grabbed onto hope with a bull dog's grip refusing to let go believing that just around the corner maybe tomorrow, maybe next week maybe next year, somebody will feel sorry for me and say I can come back to school. Sad to say, that did not happen.

I prepared myself for my own trial date realizing that I was going to have to pay for the wrong that I had done. Maybe my punishment was to never get a high school education, never get married and just raise the child that I had by someone who never really even liked me. I reached down inside of who I had become and I was determined to become the best mother in the whole wide world. I became a protector of my son. I would not allow anyone to hold him. I held him when I was feeding him, I bathed him two and three times a day, I trained him how to take naps every day. I cleaned my parent's home daily; I washed the clothes and stared at the walls all day long. I had nothing to do after my chores and I realized that school was not in the plans for me.

I would get up the next morning and start the routine all over again. I was so hurt that I hid myself behind Kerwin. I became so helpless in my emotions I forgot how to ask for help. I was so bound I forgot what a normal life entailed. All the time I was caught up in this whirlwind of pain, the jury was gathering their information to use against me - all because I made a mistake that society would not allow me to correct. How cruel to get caught the first time and not get a second chance. During this period in my life the only person that distinctly comes to mind with a word of encouragement was my Girl Scout leader Ms. Myrtle Burris. She said to me, Marsha Jo I want you to hold your head up and remember the reason why so many others are not in your predicament is because of luck - it is not because of their conduct.

According to Ms. Myrtle, I was not the only one guilty - I was the one who received the sentence. After about six months or so, I had a few visitors to come and see Kerwin. Seeing them was like a cold drink of water on a sunny hot day. I noticed they all came in to look at him as though they were looking at a body of a deceased loved one that was a distant relative, they never said he was cute or ugly, they never mentioned if he looked healthy or if he looked like Gary or if he looked like me. At this point I started an inquisition asking everyone who came to see him how he looks. No one said a word. I must admit I felt worse after they left than when they came.

I did not think my baby was ugly, but when they all left, my mother said she heard me asking the question and she said to me, "go get Kerwin and bring him to me". She said, "Look at him. Now you know how he looks, don't ask anyone else. He has ten fingers, ten toes, he is very healthy, he has no mental nor physical problems - don't you ever ask anyone else how your baby looks". I learned that lesson in about five minutes and from that day to this, how my children looked has never been an issue - I just wanted them healthy and happy. What in the world was going on with me?

I just heard that Gary had a first cousin that was spreading a rumor that Kerwin was not his baby. That was all I needed at this time in my life - I am at my lowest point. I could not believe that I was a virgin, had sex one time and got pregnant. The sad part of the commentary is that Gary acted as though he believed that Kerwin was not his baby – I wondered if this the reason why he would not speak to me or why he would not spend any time with Kerwin? Was it the reason why he never came nor called? The evidence was stacking up against me once again. Now I am real bitter; I am so upset that there were times I almost convinced myself of that lie.

After all why am I experiencing so much rejection? I don't have any more friends; I can't go to school, I can't find a job, I can't drive a car. If I went to the store, mother made me take Kerwin with me. I had no time for me.

My life was surrounded with things that I could not do and nothing of what I could do. I became so discouraged I could not forgive myself. I convinced myself that I would never have any more friends, and that nobody in Hugo liked me. I felt like I had hurt and shamed my family in the worst way. I wanted the ole Marsha Jo back where everybody knew my name. When you heard somebody say Marsha Jo, you knew that it was someone close to me. It was so amazing to me how when I was that Marsha it was easy for them to love me, but just because I made one mistake it was just as easy for those same people to hate me. How could they bless me today and curse me the next day?

It seemed like I had people all around me before I became pregnant, but as soon as I had Kerwin, they scattered like weeds in a tornado storm. I now found myself back at the family tree of my Daddy's and Mama's side. I was forced to accept my roots because of the rejection that both my parents had received from members in their family, and people in the community. I too was experiencing that same rejection. Even in this reality, it still did not eliminate the turmoil that followed me to bed nightly and the pain that I was awakened to daily. I truly felt like nobody understood me and every day of my life I felt the pressure of a trial date. I began counting down the days in my own mind because of the pain and agony build-up, and the disappointment, sorrow, unhappiness and unforgiveness of myself.

One morning I was awakened by a pain that caused every part of my being to lose control. I could not take it anymore. I was tired of the rehearsal theme song that "things were going to get better". I was bored with my rigid, strict daily routine. Kerwin almost a year old has taken his first step and still no response from Gary. Although Sharon, Gary's sister, Will, and Pat - Gary's younger brothers, were there when Kerwin took his first step. I really felt sorry for Kerwin then and twice as sorry for myself.

The next day I dressed up in my courtroom clothes and took my own self to the courthouse. I hired a lawyer who came highly recommended. His name was J.C. A Very Present Help in the times of trouble. His reputation of never losing a case preceded him. His briefcase was very unusual. It was shaped like a cross and had a red stain of blood throughout the entire cross. He specialized in the defense of the broken hearted, the sick and shut in, the least likely ones to be successful, the wounded, the hurt, the mistreated, and the rejected.

As I went through the list of charges against me, I could not believe how I could stand a chance. I was guilty as charged on all seven counts in the first degree.

The first count - guilty of a broken heart.

The second count - guilty of being sick and shut in.

The third count - guilty of being the least likely to succeed.

The fourth count - guilty of being wounded from the inside out.

The fifth count - guilty of being hurt for years.

The sixth count - guilty of being mistreated.

And the last count, I knew I would get a life sentence for this one -because it was a spirit that had kept my family in jail for generations - it was rejection.

I went down to the knee room and I summoned the Lawyer to come and take my case. I told him what I was guilty of and that I was broke spiritually, emotionally, physically, and financially. I asked if he would allow me to pay Him in payments if he could get the charges dropped against me. I promised that if He got the charges dropped, I would not be found guilty of these charges any more.

The lawyer said that he would take the case but he would like to bring in the Just Judge who was fair in all of his dealings. He said his name was Judge Unlimited Mercy. I knew that I would not have enough money to pay him so he told me the judge had some mercy that would cover all the cost.

When we entered the court room, the Just Judge was sitting high and lifted up and it looked like angels were ministering to him all around his head and in the corners of the room. When I made it to the stand, he said, "You don't have to tell me your name because I have known your name from the foundation of the world. When you passed through the waters of your trials, I did not allow them to drown you. When you went through the fiery fire, I would not allow it to consume you. It was I who up held you with my righteous right hand. So I declare this day that I find you not guilty. I have dropped all of the charges."

The Judge further stated that "The reason you could not cry while you were going through your trials is because I allowed my Son to weep for you." You were never guilty because He bore all the sin, the shame, the pain, and the brokenness on the cross. I say to you my daughter, He whom the Son of man has made free is free indeed - you are free!

Chapter 17

LIFE IN THE BIG CITY

17   *Life in the Big City!*

God once again shined His brightest light upon me. My sister Bernice had moved to Omaha, Nebraska. She was now an educator at one of the largest high schools in Omaha. So instead of sitting around home day after day, she asked mother and dad to allow me to come up and go to school with her. I had real mixed emotions because number one, I had never been away from home, and I was going to be going far away. I thought about Kenneth, Debra, Tony, Lori, Jewel, and of course mother and daddy. It wasn't like I was going to be able to walk home anytime I wanted to.

My parents agreed to allow me to visit Bernice. Bernice was always such a kind, considerate, motherly-type person. She immediately gave me my room with Kerwin. She went out and bought me all kinds of clothes, shoes, coats, you name it, I had it. She did the same thing for Kerwin. Bernice immediately took over all my responsibilities with Kerwin. She allowed me to study my books only. She bathed Kerwin, fed him, ironed his clothes, and she made sure that we both felt loved, warm, and secure.

Bernice found this nice baby sitter and she took care of Kerwin while we were at school. She charged $80.00 a month and still no word, no money, no nothing from Gary. Bernice took over financially, morally, and educationally.

C. V. (Gary's father) told me he had a sister who lived in Omaha and Bernice had taught her children. Bernice took me over to meet them. I felt a sense of acceptance as soon as I entered the door. She took Kerwin and looked at him and the first words that she said was that he looks exactly like Pot. Pot was Gary's mother's nickname, so my heart was put to ease. His cousins were all beautiful and kind people. They had shoulder length hair with strong Indian features. Donna, Jeannie, and I became real close.

When I would go visit, Donna would always carry Kerwin. He was so fat and heavy but we had a ball. I shall never forget the kindness that they showed toward Kerwin and me. I entered into Technical High school. The building was huge and intimidating. Everything was huge. The school had so many floors in it - I think the cafeteria was on the fifth floor of the building. I had never seen so many children before in my life and you must have known how I felt – like a little lost country girl. In spite of this, school felt good to me. It seemed right. I was actually happy once again. I had a smile on my face. I met new friends who were very kind to me because everybody loved Bernice.

I remember taking a school field trip where we all went to see Jessie Jackson (Operation Push). I had never experienced anything like this in my life. I thought – wow, life is greater than any problem that I had encountered in Hugo, Oklahoma. We stayed at the Ascot Hotel in Chicago, Illinois. I had never seen the inside of a hotel before and certainly had never stayed in one.

The city kids were wild. They were doing everything that I knew I could not and was not supposed to do, but I enjoyed watching them. On the route back home we went through Gary, Indiana. I knew that The Jackson Five lived there. I was so country, I actually said, "lets get the bus driver to drive by their house" hoping that I would be able to see one of them if not all of them in their yard. Well you know those city girls about laughed me off the bus. I did not know there was anything wrong with that. I thought that was normal - well it would have been in Hugo in the *Belmont Addition*.

I made it through the school year and my grades were excellent. I could not have been happier - even my voice changed. I started pronouncing my words like I was from Omaha. The one thing I shall never forget was Morning Star Baptist Church. Bernice was a member there and I went Sunday after Sunday to this church. I always believed that God was going to do something mighty in my life although I had done things out of His will. I always had a conviction about wanting to do what was right.

This particular Sunday the Pastor Z.W. Williams had brought the message and he made an altar call for those who wanted to be saved and to give their life to Christ. The choir was singing harmoniously *Just as I Am* and I had a nudge from the Lord drawing me closer and closer to Him. I got up and began walking toward the altar and it seemed like the aisle to the altar was the longest distance I had ever walked in my life. I kept walking and finally when I made it there the tears that filled my eyes had rolled down my checks to my chin and began dripping on my pink dress. I handed my hand to the Pastor and I know that day God saved me from every thing that I had gone through. I was never the same. At 16 years old, baby out of wedlock, rejection, hurt and disappointment, God sent me to Omaha, Nebraska to save my soul and, save me from myself.

The school year ended and I had met so many friends but I must be honest with you, I missed home. I missed the **Belmont Addition**, family, and friends. So we journeyed back to Hugo. It was a long ride, yet it was a ride of happiness. Kerwin even seemed happier. I had an opportunity to go to school and got my mind off of the things that stole my joy.

As soon as I entered Hugo, everybody knew that I was in town. Kerwin and I had a warm welcome. I was talking proper and Kenneth said "I know you aren't trying to talk proper you know how we talk in Hugo", he said "In one hour I am going to have you back speaking like you are from the **Belmont**, not Omaha". He was right, he started meddling like usual, and guess what, we were back fussing and meddling each other as though I had never left.

I must admit the experience that I encountered in Omaha gave me a sense of worth and a feeling that I could make it. In spite of the fact that I had attended school in Omaha, the Hugo School system said that unless I was married, I could not go back to school. So once again, I was right back where I started from. But I want you to know the power behind the words of a praying mother – they avail much - so my time spent in the Big City was worth it all.

Chapter 18

THE LIE, THE LAWYER,
AND THE LESSON

18   *The Lie, The Lawyer, and The Lesson*

For two long years the enemy tried to convince me with the lie that I was not going to be able to go back to school and that I wasn't going to be anything but an old maid with a son that I was going to have to raise by myself. I had just moved back from Omaha, Nebraska where I was able to attend school once again. The outcome of my short stay in Omaha was that I was still able to learn and that I had the ability to become successful.

I had joined church and for the first time in my life, I did not feel as though I was an outcast; I did not feel as though I should feel embarrassed every where I went; I did not have to cringe or become silent every time I heard the word baby, I did not have to accept the fact that everybody was looking down on me because I had a baby out of wedlock.

Somehow what the enemy tried to convince me of only happened when I was in Hugo. It seemed as though the memory of everything I had ever done, everything that I had ever said, was always haunting me. No matter how hard I tried to think positive, I could always hear in my ear "you are no good" – "you are worthless" – "everybody in town is talking about you" - "what you did is unforgivable".

Every time I tried to think about school, I was made to feel as though that is not the place for you. I was stuck in a town where I could not even get a job so I was forced to go get on welfare. They took me through so many changes just to get $80.00 dollars a month, but mother was determined that I was not going to bother Gary nor his family. She firmly stated that we would have to make the best out of the circumstances that we were confronted with.

I remember one Christmas Gary took a job at the Criso Plant and I really thought that he would at least buy Kerwin a toy from the five and dime store. Instead, he purchased a promise ring for his girlfriend for her Christmas gift and he never even came over Christmas to see him.

I remember one other time – Shirley Bostic, Gary's first cousin, and I walked over to Phyllis' house who had a baby by Gary's brother, Wesley. We all had our babies over just visiting and Gary came by. He was holding Kerwin when his girlfriend came over and he almost dropped him trying to give him back to me. I still wasn't getting it. I was even more confused as to why it was so hard for him to even try to act like he was somewhat concerned about his only child, and a son at that.

I had friends who were faithful to the cause. Terry Clark, James Terry, and Tony Harris. They would come over to the *Belmont Addition* to play with Kerwin or just drop by to say hello. I really felt like I had done something wrong because the enemy kept whispering in my ear, "you are being punished for having a baby out of wedlock, look at all your other friends - the fathers of their babies are taking up time with them". So once again I found myself in a stupor not knowing what to do, who to turn to, or if I should just give up on going to school altogether.

One day I had a turn around feeling in my spirit. I began to think differently, I started to act different. I felt school in every fiber of my body. My mother was a woman of God who trusted God to protect her children, to deliver her husband, to send her son home from Viet Nam, to heal her son from polio, to bless her to come out of the rut she was in - living in a one room shack with too many children, to bless her with a job to help support her family and the church. She was also believing God to bless me to be able to go back to school. She felt this was just a minor thing for God to do for her.

My mother prayed that God would send an answer and he did, he sent Don Ed Payne, a young aggressive lawyer to Hugo, Oklahoma. Attorney Payne was a 1956 graduate of Eufaula High School. At that time I was a year old. He attended Oklahoma Baptist University in Shawnee, Oklahoma from 1946-1958, University of Tulsa, receiving his B .A. in History and Political Science in 1959 which at the time I was four years old and he received his L.L.B. in 1962, I completed my first grade and started the second grade. Don Ed was Associate District Judge for Choctaw County in Hugo, Oklahoma and he was District Attorney for the 17th District of Oklahoma from 1965-1971. He also practiced private law.

He was devoted primarily to the defense of criminal cases in Hugo, Oklahoma from 1971-1995 and in 1972-73, mother presented the facts to him and he said "I will take the case". Attorney Payne took the case for a fee of $50.00. Once he did this, the heat was on. Mr. Payne could not believe that the town was so far behind the times. He wondered how a system could be so lop-sided as to make the mother of a child leave and not obtain an education and allow the father to go on to finish high school.

Mr. Payne was very upset with my situation and challenged the school district to present their reasoning. Mr. Payne was shrewd in his thinking. He set the court date on a Saturday and the officials did not show up. We won the case! The school district did not want to fight the case because they had never had anyone to challenge the rule. The sad part of the commentary was that I had many friends that I knew who got pregnant under the old law and they were never able to go back to school to get their diploma.

Starting in 1973, the law was changed. An article appeared in the Hugo Daily news. I made the news! The paper read, "Akins Vs Hugo High School". I was able to walk back through the doors of the school that the school district said I could never come back to unless I was married. When you have God on your side, you know that when man says no, God says yes, and it is so.

I must admit that I was very grateful to be able to go back to school. The only sad part of going back was that my class that I had started the first grade with graduated without me. Although I was there in spirit, I was absent in body. Once again my friends were so excited for me that they never excluded me from anything that I could be a part of. They always remembered the bond that we developed over the years and the relationship that we were able to keep in tact. I went on back to school, kept my studies up, and made good grades.

I shall never forget Mrs. Estella Grant, Kerwin's babysitter. She was a kind Christian woman who was what I needed in my life at the time. I had to pick him up every day, complete my homework, feed, bathe, and get Kerwin ready for bed so that we could start the routine all over again the next day. I kept this routine until I finished high school. Challenging though it was, I must say that the experience was good for me.

By now Gary was in the United States Army and married. When he got married, I realized that whatever I thought, wasn't, and whatever I thought could have been - never happened. Kerwin never received any financial support, moral support, or any type of encouragement from his father. Gary was not even there when Kerwin graduated from high school. Kerwin led his graduating class into the graduating ceremony as Kerwin Dawand Akins. In spite of Gary's lack of participation in the life of his son, I thank God for sending Don Ed Payne into our lives.

Don Payne remained in Hugo and became the Honorable Don Ed Payne, Judge of Hugo. I regret however, that as I write these lines there is sadness in my heart because he has a terminal illness, and is not doing very well. One thing that I am appreciative of is that he was able to make a difference in my life and every other girl's life after me who became pregnant. They were all able to go back to school and earn their High School Diploma all because of the most Honorable Don Ed Payne.

Don Ed Payne was an avid golfer, and enjoyed running and participated in several marathons. He was a member of the Oklahoma Bar Association and the Texas Bar Association. Don Ed received several awards including the Oklahoma Bar Association Courageous Advocate Award in 1989, Oklahoma Criminal Defense Lawyers Association, Lord Erskine Award in 1994, the American Civil Liberties Union of Oklahoma and The Angie Debo Award in 1994.

Don Ed also lectured and instructed at seminars and trainings for trial lawyers (primarily in the areas of criminal defense and defense of death penalty cases) sponsored by the various legal organizations. He also served as a CLEET certification instructor for peace officers, and until the time that he became will, a volunteer adjunct instructor for Eastern Oklahoma State College, teaching primarily Criminal Justice and corrections classes, which was my major in college.

On the back of his obituary are inscribed the following words which sums up the Honorable Don Ed Payne's life in 38 words.

What Cancer Cannot Do

It cannot cripple Love
It cannot shatter Hope
It cannot erode Faith
It cannot destroy Peace
It cannot kill Friendship
It cannot suppress Memories
It cannot evade the Soul
It cannot steal Eternal Life
It cannot conquer the Spirit

One thing I know is that I learned the lesson, even though it was a long drawn out process. The questions would come and I did not know how to answer them, then the pop quiz of all time was given and the presenting issue was knowing who you are and being who you are. I then experienced the trials of remorse, rejection, regret which hung over my head. I also had to deal with the temptations of staying strong, not to get involved in dead-end relationships.

I must admit that God kept me when I did not even realize that I needed someone to keep me, to protect me, and to console me. God was there all the time, pulling at my heart strings telling me to hang in there, urging me not to give up, whispering in a quiet voice saying, "hold on, help is on the way". When I made it to the end of that journey, I realized that it was God who was there all the time. It was He who encouraged my mother by assuring her that "because you have been faithful, I am going to bless you in your darkest hour".

I learned a lesson that nobody can ever make me forget. It took me a long time, but I passed the test. What I discovered is, you sometimes have to go through many trials to get to what God has for you. When you take matters in your own hand and try to fix them without consulting Him first, you fail every time. I recognized that there is no failure in God. I can say that through it all, it was worth the pain, and the struggle. The wounds that are now healed scars are reminders that it took a long time to heal, but it does not hurt anymore.

Every time I try to remember how bad I hurt at the age of 15, the pain will not resurface. So here I am in a place where I have learned that you cannot out run a lie, you cannot chase it down and kill it, but it will slow down and eventually it will die. I learned that whatever you go through in life, you can overcome it if you don't give in to it.

If you really want to make a change in your life, ask God to change you. If you will do this, everything and everyone that comes your way will fall in line with who you are and not with whom and what they want you to become. If you can stay true and obedient to your parents, if you can know that your worth is more precious than silver and gold, if you can believe that no matter how bad you want to do something - if it goes against the way you were raised, if it goes against what is right, don't do it. In spite of how you feel about yourself, if the feeling makes you feel less than who God says you are, just know the enemy is attempting to take away from your true identity.

If you can believe what God has said about you, know that He is going to complete the work that He began in you until the day of His return.

Always know that beauty is only as deep as the last layer of skin on your body. I say to you, run as though you are in a race and don't stop until you run into the place, the person, and the purpose that God has for you. I say to each of you - I heard the Lie, I thank God for the Lawyer, and I learned the Lesson.

Reflections On The Life Of A Most Notable Man

Don Ed Payne
Susan Spencer Payne

Don Ed was one of the most gifted orators I ever heard. He could purr at recalcitrant judges, nudging them into unwilling agreement or he could deliver thunderbolts like Zeus, daring the audience to differ.

He was raised in an Oklahoma fundamentalist religious tradition. Whatever else Don Ed thought of that, he often attributed his power of oratory to the training he received in his youth in the Baptist Church. Now those powerful words are forever still.

As Clarence Darrow, the famous lawyer once said: "A truer, greater, gentler, kindlier soul has never lived and died."

Don Ed was a talented and gifted lawyer. He certainly had the option of being a "tall tower lawyer" and selling his time to a series of corporate masters. Instead he toiled for decades in the courtrooms of this nation, as the attorney for the little guy.

Don Ed was a foot soldier in the endless struggle to keep America free to prevent our government from inching past protection and into tyranny. When a lawyer chooses this path, he often pays a price in personal security and wealth.

The French philosopher Albert Camus made as good an answer as any to the question, "Does this process from cradle to grave to which we all so desperately cling have any meaning?" In his essay the Myth of Sisyphus, he uses Sisyphus as a metaphor for modern man. Sisyphus, according to Homer, was condemned by Zeus to an eternity of rolling a heavy boulder up a hill, only to see it roll back again. Camus uses this example of endless vain labor in order to ask and answer the question: does this life have meaning? He argues that if we look over the millennia, it makes little difference whether we live one day or a hundred years, whether we are a famous general or a nameless foot soldier but he argues that the meaning of life is not discovered in the centuries, but in the millisecond, and that it is expressed and discovered through kindness. Kindness has its own intrinsic meaning. Surely my husband and friend, Don Ed Payne is an exhibit of a singular life of kindness and self-sacrifice which demonstrates that meaning.

When asked why he undertook unpopular paths, he said that he always hated bullies, and that majorities were just another variety of bullies. Don Ed understood that the genius of Philadelphia was our then unique system which provided for majority rule but established certain boundaries in which the majority could not tyrannize the minority. Don Ed often expressed that he was glad that his right of free speech was codified in the Bill of Rights, but that he believed the right of man to express himself without governmental or majority approval was a natural right which had existed precisely as long as humans had possessed the power of speech. Don Ed Payne gave his life to public service.

I submit to you that his greatest contribution was not as an elected District Attorney nor as a District Judge, it was during his decades as a stand up trial lawyer, litigating cases for the damned, the unpopular, the unwashed, and the unwelcome that his light shone most brightly.

Chapter 19

POP TRUCK

19 _Pop Truck_

Cast your bread upon the waters, For
you will find it after many days.

ECCLESIASTES 11: 1

Who is that charismatic, good looking, smooth-talking, sharp dressed guy with that pool stick in his hand? He had on a pair of brown slacks with a brown sweater that had burnt orange stripes intertwined in the sleeves that ballooned out. Every time he moved the stick or shot the pool ball, his sleeves would show the burnt orange stripe.

He stood approximately 5 ft 7 inches tall. His weight appeared to be about 145 pounds. He was long-waisted which made him appear taller than he actually was. He had freckles on his face, but behind the freckles were cute well shaven sideburns that met at the end of his jaw line. He had short stubby fingers; his eyes were shaped like quarter moons that danced behind his long eyelashes.

His mustache was trimmed perfectly and rested over his top lip like it was never disheveled or rumpled. His teeth were strong but crooked at the bottom. On the front tooth was a gold open-faced crown. When he smiled you could see how handsome he really was. Instantly I knew that he was not from Hugo, Oklahoma.

He was different; he was a city boy, full of class, and style. He was concentrating on his pool game. Every now and then he would wave the pool stick with such skill that it was like being entertained at a pool show; then he would stick the head of the pool stick into the chalk to make the balls scatter easily. You could tell that he knew something about the game.

All of a sudden Lonnie Ray, whom we called the "Godfather", called me over and said, Marsha Jo, come here, I would like for you to meet someone. I could not believe it - I was going to get the opportunity to meet this new guy in town first. Lonnie said, "Truckee I would like for you to meet Marsha - this is Kenneth Akins' sister". Kenneth was my favorite brother, so immediately I started thinking that Kenneth knew him too! I came back out of the ten second dream world when I heard the most beautiful voice and looked into the cutest eyes, and witnessed the nicest smile that I had ever seen.

I was mesmerized when he took my hand and said, "Hello, it's nice to meet you". When I came to myself, I said in my most proper voice, "Hi! It's nice to meet you too". He invited me to sit in the booth with him so we could become more acquainted with each other.

I must admit I have never felt like I was as special as I did at that very moment. I had just won the case to enter back into high school and I was determined that I was going to graduate from high school. My son Kerwin had a wonderful sitter, Mrs. Estella Grant. I had not been out in ages because I was taking care of my responsibilities and studies, but God ordained this meeting. We sat there and talked for hours. He offered to give me a ride home with his fraternity brother Victor Walker. I remember how thoughtful he was. I had forgotten Kerwin's pampers in the car, and he brought them all the way back to me. I remember him knocking on the door and Daddy asking, "who is it?". He said, Darrel Jordan, sir - "Marsha left her son's pampers in the car, and I would like to return them". Little did I know that he would become my husband, Kerwin's father, my parent's son–in law, and Akins' brother-in-law. You talking about God performing a miracle, or that he works in mysterious ways! I was so impressed that on that night a new attitude was birthed inside of me.

I began to reflect back over all the things that I had gone through- all the trials, all the disappointments, all the heartbreaks, all the lonely and dark days, now I was actually looking through the tunnel and the first time in years I saw light. I was able to see how he looked; I remembered how he carried himself, how he used choice words that did not seem like they were implausible or made up. All I could do as my eyelids gave way to deep sleep was to say "Thank You Lord"! I had a smile on my face and a song in my heart.

The more Truck and I continued to converse with each other, I found out just how charming and interesting he really was. He was always fascinating and delightful to be around. He was very positive and he knew who he was. He had one brother, Rodney Craig, his sisters were- Joyce, Jo Ann, Janice, Wynona, Georgette, and Tracey. His mother's name was Frankie and his father's name was Joe Willie. I thought one more ball in the basket - my middle name was Jo!

He also told me how he played basketball and the school newspaper had interviewed when he scored 34 points in a tournament game. I was simply fascinated with Pop Truck so I wanted to know how he ended up with a nick name like Pop Truck. He shared with me that everyday when he came home with his mother, he would be drinking a soda pop. When the neighbor Clarence Holman saw him, he told him he was going to turn into a pop. So in order to keep his reputation up, he would steal pop off the pop truck when the truck would make its rounds to the local grocery stores. I thought "wow!" he is so daring.

I was captivated with this guy called Pop Truck. When I introduced him to my father, the first thing he said was, "you have been talking about this Pop Truck- I thought he was a diesel, he is just a little truck. You have to know that my father and Truck were the same height.

By now Gary wasn't even saying hello to me or paying any attention to Kerwin. At that point I did not care anymore. God in his infinite wisdom, in his timely manner, knew and supplied just what I needed, exactly when I needed it. He had sent a ray of hope into my life for every cloud that dimmed out my hope. He sent Darrel Pop Truck Jordan to rekindle that spark that would eventually be ignited into a flame identified as love. I went to school on Monday with a brand new attitude. I concentrated on my studies and kept loyal to my dream of finishing high school.

The next week I received a beautiful hot pink envelop with green stationary to match. The letter was from Darrel E. Jordan addressed to Marsha J. Akins at 1201 East Medlock Street in Hugo, Oklahoma. I thought the *Belmont Addition* will never be the same. Here this guy was a freshman in college and I was a senior in high school and I was getting mail from a college campus. I read the letter over and over and then I finally found my friend Sharon and let her read my letter. The one line that I shall never forget was the one line where he wrote, "Marsha, it is inevitable that we will be together". All I knew was being together sounded great, and I didn't have a clue what the word inevitable meant.

Sharon and I went straight to the Library at Hugo High and took down the huge dictionary and began to thumb through the pages looking for the word inevitable. We finally came upon it and the definition said "not to be avoided; sure to happen: certain to come".

I almost lost it in the Library. The Librarian came by to remind us that we were too loud. I had to leave out of the library. I could not believe it, but it set real well on the inside as I asked myself - could this be really real? I was so happy. Now everything in my life had meaning, I had purpose, I had destiny. I could taste my future and I denounced my past. My hope dressed up in the finest linen. My mind did a metamorphic turn around. I was on my way. School became more exciting to me because all I could think about now was I am going to go to college.

I remember talking to my Aunt Willie Mae who is now deceased - she encouraged me to go on to college and that there was plenty of every thing there - plenty of people, new places to see, and tons of learning. She said I am sure you will be able to get married. Just because one apple is spoiled it doesn't mean that you have to hate apples now. I graduated from Hugo High – the same school district that said you can't go here any longer. We won the case Akins verses Hugo High School. Even though I was a year late, I still led the graduating senior class of 1974 in the baccalaureate and the commencement exercises. The theme song was We're Loyal to You Hugo High. The school's mascot was Hugo Water Buffaloes. The school colors were black and gold.

My dear readers, the happiest day of my life was that day when I walked across the stage and they called out my name, Marsha Jo Akins. My faithful friends who I had started out with were there once again cheering me on. What a blessing from God! I remember after graduation going in telling mother that I wanted to go to college. She said "that is a wonderful idea". Her next words were "pack Kerwin's clothes and remember all that I taught you". (My Blessing) I was so excited to have finished high school and now getting ready to go college that I did not think twice about leaving home.

I remember asking God for three more blessings and they were: Lord bless me with a husband who will love and not mistreat Kerwin, who will love me and my family, and bless me with a degree. The Lord was so full of compassion. I trusted him to do exactly what I asked and He did!!!

Chapter 20

THE BLESSING, THE BAG, AND THE BABY

20   The Blessing, The Bag, and The Baby

"I will bless those who bless you, And I
will curse him who curses you.

GENESIS 12; 3

What is this thing called blessing? What is this thing called Grace? What is this thing called Mercy? What is thing called Favor? All I know is that these things found me, wrapped themselves around me, gave me a Sonny Listen upper cut, a Cassias Clay shuffle and turned my entire life around in a matter of months.

I caught a ride to Edmond, Oklahoma and now Kerwin and I are on our way to the campus of Central State University. I remember dressing up in my best outfit, and putting Kerwin's cute little burnt orange corduroy suit on him. I had greased and brushed his hair, and lotioned him down - he looked so cute. He was a quiet little fellow - a kid of few words. He never really smiled a lot, but he had my teeth and my smile. When he did smile, he looked so much like me. He was very obedient but he always acted as though he had a lot on his mind.

We went into the Financial Aide Director's office. I sat Kerwin in the seat next to me and Mr. Massey, the Director of Finance finally came out and asked me how could he help me? Back then I was so wrapped up in horoscope that if I looked at you, I could tell what your zodiac sign was. I asked him was his birthday in March and he looked at me and smiled and asked me how did I know that? He said, "As a matter of fact, my birthday is March 25". I told him my birthday was March 28. I knew right then that I was in like Flynn.

Mr. Massey had on a light brown suit, his hair was a chestnut brown that was curly on the top and he wore wire-framed eye glasses. He looked at me with a crooked smile and asked me, "What can I do for you today?" I told him that this was my son Kerwin and that I wanted to go to college and that I did not have any money. He looked at me with a smile on his face as to say, "How are you going to do that?" As he looked at Kerwin, I became very defensive. I told him that all I had was a blessing that my mother gave me by telling me that I could come and that I could make it. I had one bag with both our clothes in it, and this is my baby. I told him that I caught a ride up here and I have no where to go and no money to get back home. So Mr. Massey told me that he would give me a loan for one semester and allow me to live in the marriage housing if I maintained a 2 point grade average. I could not believe my ears. I was really going to be able to go to college.

I enrolled in 15 hours not knowing what all that meant. As I was walking out of the Administration Building, I met two girls who were coming in as I was going out. It was Myra Walker who was just as dark as I was. She had long cold black hair that graced her shoulders as though it was a piece of protection. The other one was Willie C. Gaines, who was a real petite girl with huge pretty eyes and a warm smile. They introduced themselves and asked if this was my son. I told them yes, and that I was from Hugo and I was going to go to college.

They asked me who was going to baby-sit Kerwin while I was in class. I told them I was going to take him to class with me. They both looked at each other and kind of smiled and asked me to look at my class schedule. They then said, "Let's revise our schedule". Myra said, "Marsha, you take the class at eight and Willie will take the class at nine and I will take the class at ten - then we will all baby-sit Kerwin. I thought, "Wow God, you are so awesome!"

I finally moved into my apartment. Kerwin had his own room with a twin bed in it and I had my room. I can still remember my kitchen. It had a red table with iron legs with 4 red chairs to match. The living room was tan and chocolate stripped with wood sidings on the couch. The chair was a rocker with two wooden end tables and a coffee table. Life could not have been better. College life was great. There were so many people, so many assignments, and so many stores to go to - just like Aunt Willie Mae had said.

Then guess who I meet up with again - yes, you are right, Darrel Pop Truck Jordan. He was such a man now. He did not even look the same. He would come by and take Kerwin to the games, or he would just stop by to say hello, and sometimes he would just stop by to see if everything was alright. I remember one day after class, he and I were just talking and Darrel bet me that he could out run me backwards and I could run forward. Well, the bet was on. Guess what - yep - he won. He was so much fun.

Kerwin fell in love with him. Then one day Truck took me back to the letter he wrote when he said that it was inevitable that we would be together. Well, one day while walking on the campus, he was so fascinated with my perseverance and my drive to succeed in spite of the obstacles that I was confronted with - he told me I am going to marry you. To all of my readers, you know that blew my mind. I could not believe my ears. God again had not forgotten to shine on me with his rays of love. By now I had completed an entire year of school. Kewrin was now in Canterbury Nursery and my studies were coming along fine.

It was at this time that I realized that Mr. Massey did not have the heart to tell me that he did not believe that I was going to make it - that's why he only offered me financial aid for one semester. Well, too bad, too sad. I could smell the spring of my life and I anticipated summer. I wrapped myself up into autumn and I put on my thickest coat for winter, and I made it!

Kerwin was the only kid on campus so everybody spoiled him rotten. Boy - those were the days.

Finally the mission had been completed. I felt as though everything that I had gone through was necessary for me to accept and to continue to move forward - and that's exactly what I did.

Chapter 21

COLLEGE LIFE

21   *College Life*

I had met so many new friends my first week in school. My classes were interesting, but I had never been in a class that had so many students in one class. Despite this fact, I loved learning, so I was taking everything in. I remember my Humanities teacher very vividly - her name was Ms. Ethel Quickle. Her looks and demeanor were that of a college professor.

She was an older lady with a small frame. Her hair was blonde and she wore it up in a French roll. Her voice was quiet but captivating as she explained the lessons she prepared for the class. I remember her class was in the Liberal Arts Building, and all the students on the yard called it the L.A. building.

I still remember how beautiful the campus was then. I had always wanted to live in the dormitory, but I had a baby and could not. My friends who lived in the dorm either lived in West Hall or Murdaugh Hall. East Hall and Thatcher Hall were the dorms for boys only. The Communication Building was centrally located in the middle of the campus and the only black professor in that department was Mr. Willard Pitts. He was always there for us, coaching and encouraging us to stay focused and not to forget what our purpose was in coming to college.

The other building for classes was called Old North and we were blessed to have yet another black male professor, Dr. Malcolm Coby, who taught Special Education Classes. Mrs. Linda Matthews, the black counselor, was always there prompting us to take the right classes and making sure we had the necessary requirements to graduate on our target date. The campus was huge, but I managed to find all my classes and work hard.

I remember meeting an attractive, tall, slender lady one day as I was traveling the yard – by the name of Diane Hughes. She I had a lot of fun together. Diane would come over and help with Kerwin. She also worked at this department store downtown Edmond called McCall's. Every time there was a sale, she would call and let me know and most often she would buy Kerwin some of the cutest outfits. Diane loved children, so this was just normal for her.

When she would alert her friends and me of the upcoming sales, she would always give us direct instructions, such as "Do not wear any hair rollers in your hair, no head scarves, and no house shoes". We would just laugh at her because we felt we had arrived since we were now living in the City. You would have to know Diane's personality in order to not get upset with her when she made these types of statements. Her nickname on the yard was Miss Clean.

Diane had a wonderful personality and a beautiful smile; shoulder length hair, graceful in her body language, a shrewd business lady, and was a very caring young lady. When I met her I was waiting on my loan papers to come through, and because I had a baby to care for, Diane fronted the money to me until the loan came in. I shall always remember this kind act because I did not ask her to do this, and she did not have to do it. She did not know me at all. Still today we have kept our relationship in tact.

After the first semester I had friends everywhere. My apartment was the spot. It seemed as though I never ran out of food. Kerwin was getting the attention that he needed from every one and I was able to participate in some of the school functions.

I remember joining this organization called the Alpha Angels. My angel name was Queen of Spades. I distinctively remember one of the times we were all getting ready to go to one of the campus dances. I was over in the dormitory with some of the other angels and everyone was getting their outfits together. The girls who could sew were cutting out their patterns and sewing their outfits together. You know I did not know how to sew so everyone wanted me to just be the life of the party and keep everybody awake laughing and talking and they would do the sewing.

During the preparation, they decided to take a food break so they all went to McDonald's to purchase our food. I stayed behind and decided to make everyone proud of me. I decided to sew my outfit together that they had already cut out. Boy did I sew it together alright. I sewed the back in the front and the front in the back. When they returned after they stopped laughing, they told me to take the stitch puller and take all of it apart. Their recommendation was for me to stick to entertaining, and they would do the sewing.

We made it through all of that and we were down to the final hour of the party. The question was, "who was going to win Miss Alpha Angel". And guess who won, you got that right, I was selected by the Alpha's themselves.

I won Miss Alpha Angel my first year on the campus. My home boy Larry Johnson was the president of the Alpha Phi Alpha

Fraternity was my escort. I guess my personality paid off after all. College life was more than what I could even imagine. There were so many Alpha Angels in the organization, and every one of them was so gifted and talented. Barbara Hawkins could sing like a bird, and she was called Hawk. Linda Johnson was called Mellow Yellow, Willie C. was called Stroud, Barbara Johnson was called Lil Barbara, Diane Gordon was called Sweet D, Betty Williams was known as Foxy Betty, and Eudora was known as The Mind Blowing Queen. Those were the days of clean fun and innocence.

I found myself the most happiest when I actually realized that life had another side to it other than Hugo. Although everything was not peaches and cream, I sure learned how to take the bitter with the sweet. By now I am enrolled in another semester of school. My life had turned for the better. I hardly ever thought about what I had gone through, Gary was a thing of the past.

I zipped myself up in my new-found freedom and I forgot all about what I did not have. I began concentrating on the things I had now. I forgot about what was going on in my old hometown and I began to appreciate the town in which I now lived. I realized how crippled I truly had become. I did not have a drivers license so someone had to take me everywhere I went. I always made it to where I needed to go. I did not have a job but I cannot remember wanting for anything. I continued to study, take care of my son, and I never flunked out of college.

My brother Kenneth was there and we were very close so life was just great. When Kenneth's College Diploma came in the mail, I was even more determined to graduate from the same college as my Big Brother Kenneth Craig. I was on a mission to enjoy my new life and graduate from college.

Chapter 22

THE AKINS FAMILY

22   _The Akins Family_

R. J. Sr.

Mr. Black, Uncle Black, Mr. Blackman, Blackie, Little Man, and Daddy - these are the names that described my father on the outside, but real words are limited in definition to describe the man I called Daddy.

I would start out by saying that he was a little man with a great big heart. Daddy was one of the most tender-hearted persons that I have ever known in my life. He lived to be the ripe old age of 83. He would tell us his birthday by saying he was born on the 14th day of April, in 1919. He was married to my mother for 57 years. Although his health was failing him daily, I believe he was determined to give Mother one more year. Daddy was bed-ridden for five years and died 6 days after their 57th anniversary.

Daddy loved people, family, and hard work. He did not understand a lazy man. He taught us that a real man knew how to pursue money and make it, and that work builds character. Daddy taught his sons how to work. He made each of us get up out of the bed early in the morning. You could never lie around in his house. He turned the lights out, locked the doors, and made sure all of us were in our perspective places before he went to bed. He was the first one to get up and he was the last one to go to bed.

Daddy made us go to church although he only visited occasionally. My father could quote scripture and learned to live by most of them. We knew not to give mother any trouble when it came to church because we would suffer the consequences when we got home.

Daddy accepted Jesus Christ as his personal Savior September 6, 1992 and united with Miracle Temple Church of God In Christ. He rededicated his life in 1997 to the Lord before his death in 2003. He wanted to make sure that he had done all that he possibly could to leave a legacy with his offspring and be in right fellowship with the Lord. Rev. Leonard Fisher, his brother-in-law, conducted Daddy's funeral at First Baptist Church, the only church in Hugo that could accommodate the 700 attendees. What a testimony of the life he lived.

As soon as one of the children got a job, daddy deducted his portion. He said we could not pay his rent, but he was teaching us how to learn how to pay our rent so that we would not continue to high-tail back home every time we hit a bump in the road. Although, we were grown and gone, Daddy's rule never changed. You just didn't walk in his house and touch things without permission and you certainly did not turn on his air conditioner which was a window unit. Daddy claimed he did not like refrigerator air blowing on him.

You also did not turn his television on because he wanted his electric bill to be the same every month and you certainly could not whip his grandchildren in his house. Daddy would tell you, don't come to my house to show off - you should have whipped them before you left home. He would take the belt and tell you that you were the one who needed to be whipped.

My Daddy gave each of his grandchildren a new pronunciation of their names, but they each knew who he was talking to. The grandsons whose father's totally neglected them, called him Daddy, some of his grandchildren called him Grandpa, Grandpa Black and still some of them called him Uncle Black. But believe me, they knew very well that he was truly their grandpa.

The last time my father was able to walk was at his 50th wedding anniversary. He had on a black tuxedo with a gold vest that Linda Ray, the mother of his grandson, Darion Keith, rented for him. Daddy kept his eyes on the prize which was the gold tree that was filled with greenbacks. You would have to know how much money meant to him to appreciate this gift. My father was well known in the town and certainly in the *Belmont Addition*. He touched the lives of many with his sense of humor, his generosity, and his tender heart. He is truly missed, but what he imparted into the lives of his family shall forever live in our hearts, mind, actions, and deeds.

Mrs. Bobbie the Trainer

Mrs. Bobbie, Bobbie Jean, Mother Akins, Sister Bob, and Mother are the names that my mother is affectionately called. Mother has a quiet, easy-going spirit about her. She never makes waves; she is not confrontational; she never tries to prove a lie; she will ignore almost everything unless it is concerning the things of God.

My mother is not a sensitive person. I have never seen her drop a tear except at funerals. She loves her children, but will be the first to tell you that she hates the wrong in them. Mother let us know early in life that it did not matter whether we liked her or not because some of us she did not like. But that she loved every last one of us. My mother made sure we were in church every Sunday from sun up until the sun went down. She taught us how to work and would not accept anything that was half done. Mother never whined about the hand that she was dealt, she just played her hand until she won. So whatever life dealt her, she took it like a woman and trusted God to bring her out.

Mother was only 15 years of age when my father married her. Three weeks after their marriage, mother became bed-ridden with a bad case of arthritis. When she was able to get up, she never mentioned it again. Mother told me that she had married my father and she knew he had a tender heart, loved helping people and he also loved to gamble. There was one thing she knew for certain, that he was going to make sure that his family had a roof over their head and that they were going to have food to eat and the necessities of life - everything else to him was not important.

Mother recalls that right before she accepted Jesus Christ as her Lord and Savior, she was about to throw the towel in on the marriage, but God came in and blessed her with a job. She told God that she wanted her children to have more, and she promised to be a blessing to the church. Mother kept her vow and has remained at the same church for over 53 years. The Lord has blessed her children more than she even knew how to ask or think.

Growing up, Mother was a strong disciplinarian. She said what she meant and she meant what she said. If she said she was going to whip you before the next day if we did not complete our chores, you were going to get the whipping if it meant pulling the covers back at 11:00 at night. When we would ask mother if we could go play with our friends she would have us to go get the Bible and read to her the scripture that says "withdraw thy foot from thy neighbor's house lest he will become tired of you and he will hate you". So we would go put the bible up and we knew what the answer was. Sometimes we would want our friends to come over and Mother would tell us nobody is coming in today and nobody is going out - you are going to learn how to play with your own brothers and sisters.

Mother hated bragging, boastful spirits. She would whip you quicker for that than anything else. I remember spending the night with my grandparents on my father's side and they gave me a mailman bank and put money in it. Mama Mag made me a cute dress and I went back home to brag about what I had. I looked at the food they were eating and I said you all are eating rice again we are having pork chops. Mother heard me and she said from this day you are going to eat the same thing they are eating and your bank and your dress is going to stay at your grandmother's. You know my Mother did not give second chances when she had explained her position clearly.

I remember Mother paying for my sister Debra and me to take piano lessons and God once again open a door for us to be able to take the lessons from Mrs. Pina. She wanted to know if I would like to sell chocolate candy bars as a fund raiser. Those candy bars were made by the same company that groups can purchase today for fund raisers. I gladly said yes and when I said "yes", I knew better. I took the candy home and my brothers and sisters and I devoured every last one of them. Mother said well, there is your piano lesson money. I can't pay for both, and since the candy is gone I have to pay for it. So in that case I wish she had whipped me but she did not I just did not get to take piano lessons anymore.

My Mother was blessed with the gift of wisdom and she knew how to deal with people on all levels. She told her children that "when you have children, be careful what you laugh at, because the same thing that will make you laugh will make you cry. She said when you agree with your children and do not tell them right from wrong or when they are two and walk across your feet it doesn't hurt that bad but when they are 22 and walk across your heart, it will almost kill you.

We were never allowed to play ends against the middle when it came to our parents. They were together when it came to raising us. We never told Daddy on Mother and we never told Mother on Daddy. My Mother taught us how to love and respect our Father by example. When she prepared dinner, My Father sat at the head of the table; we blessed the food and My Daddy got the first dipping of everything. She said that we were not going to run out of food, but Daddy had to make the money so we could all eat so he was served first.

My Mother loved the Lord and she did not care who knew it. When we would come home and she was on her way to church she said I will see you when I get back and if I miss you I will see you the next time. I know that she sounds different well she was and I thank God for her. Mrs. Bobbie, the Trainer.

Ruby Jewel

Ruby Jewel is my oldest sister. She was raised by our grandmother, Maggie and Papa Jay. Ruby Jewel is my daddy's oldest child by his first marriage. Jewel has always been around us. She had beautiful hair, beautiful skin, and a laugh like none other. Growing up, Jewel used to have me scratch her scalp it seemed like for hours. She always had good food at her house. She was always so much fun and we loved hanging around her house.

When I became pregnant, she was right in my corner. She never made me feel like I was less than anyone else. She took me to purchase my gowns and house shoes for the hospital stay. She taught me how to purchase the Mother's Friend's oil and how to use it to eliminate the stretch marks that came with having a baby.

Ruby Jewel was right there during the entire 12 hours of my labor and delivery. She stood by my side as two stones and she was precious to me in the hour that I needed her the most. Jewel would give us a ride to school every day, and she used to love to take all of us to Paris, Texas with her. She made that 25 mile trip one way at least 4 times a month.

Jewel was an over-protective aunt and she believed that you should take care of your responsibility. One day she dropped Kerwin and me off from the store. When she pulled away from the curb real slow, Kerwin sort of fell down by the car. Jewel was a nervous wreck. She kept calling and checking on Kerwin. We finally took him to the hospital to find that there was nothing wrong with Kerwin. Jewel could not believe it and told the doctor that she had run over him. The doctor told her with his stern voice, "I said you did not run over the baby. He is okay". My friends, Terry and Booley walked to the hospital and asked how bad Jewel's car was dented. That is the only thing that made her laugh again and that gave her peace of mind knowing that Kerwin was okay.

Jewel had eight children, and 9 brothers and one sister. There is no doubt that she knew a little bit about children because she was the oldest sibling. We had a great relationship and often times, my children would tease me saying that I look like Aunt Jewel Akins. Jewel was truly a precious jewel in my life and because of her time and effort, we have remained in a sister-friend relationship.

R. J. Jr.

R. J. was my daddy's first son. He was the exact replica of my father in looks, size, and build. He was a fun loving brother; always happy, in a good mood and he loved family. R. J. could play the harmonica as though he had taken lessons all his life. He was the best drummer in the entire school district. R J. was called "Ache" because every time you saw him, he had a toothache, headache or a heart ache. Something would be aching on him.

I can remember R. J. always coming to town picking my sister Debra and me up and taking us to the country with him and his girlfriend. He would always tell us when he was ready to leave the *Belmont* that he was going to have to go the Ponderosa because the High Chaparral was too small. We did not know what he meant then but when we arrived in the country we understood perfectly well what he was saying to us. As far as the naked eye could see were trees and woods.

I shall never forget when R. J. Jr., returned to the States from the army. He returned home to find that the little sister that he left was pregnant and was ready to become a mother. R. J. was so upset that he went looking for Gary. I am so glad that he was not able to locate him because he was very upset with the whole situation but he never changed toward me. He reassured me that it was all right and to hold my head up and that I was going to make it.

Although R. J. was only 43 years old when he died, I shall never forget how he cherished me as his little sister. He felt that one of his biggest aches was that I had so many hurdles to go through and I was too young to have so many issues thrown my way. I thank God that R. J. was afforded the opportunity to see me graduate from High School, College, and get married before he passed away.

Chapter 23

THE AKINS FAMILY CONTINUES

23 _The Akins Family Continues_

Bernice

Bernice, the oldest child by mother and daddy. was always a great sister. She loved her siblings to the point that she paved the way for us to make it in life. She was a trail-blazer and whatever she touched, it prospered.

Bernice's name means victorious and she was just that! Bernice was chosen "Miss Personality" while in college. She had a great attitude about everything; she was not a complainer - she just did what she had to do. I can remember when she found out after only being gone for four years that her little sister was pregnant. It was devastating for Bernice, but she never said a negative word, she just kept trying to figure out what she could do to help make the situation better for the entire family.

Bernice had graduated from college and had landed a great job as a school counselor and teacher at Technical High School in Omaha, Nebraska. She suggested that I come stay with her so I could finish the academic year out after having Kerwin. I accepted her invitation and moved to Omaha. Bernice took Kerwin as her own and all I had to do was concentrate on my studies. She taught me how to feel good about myself once again and applauded me in everything that I did. She told me how proud she was of me and that I was still just as smart as I was when I had to leave school. She introduced me to great people who thought I was really fun and great to be around. She bought me new clothes and shoes and she allowed me to be 16 and not have to spend my every waking moment with Kerwin. Still today I am most grateful for all the things she did for me. I am the teacher that I am today because I believed her report and followed her example.

Arbrey

Arbrey is my second oldest brother and he is the family member who has always been a mover and a shaker. He has always wanted the top of the line - nothing but the best. Although his energy and desire to achieve has caused some to misunderstand him, Arbrey's heart is as big as Texas - so much like my father's.

Arbrey is the brother who wanted his family to succeed in life and he did not have a problem helping you get there. His only requirement was that you had to know where you were going. Arbrey set all kinds of records. He was the first to get married, the first to leave home, the first to go to Viet Nam and make it home safely, and the first to buy a new car. He was also the first to purchase a new home. You name it - Arbrey did it.

Arbrey had a no-nonsense attitude about accomplishing your purpose. I remember when he came home from Viet Nam he was very angry. He could not understand how he left his little sister at home to find upon his return that I was still a little girl except I was pregnant. He was terrified, however, when I had the baby, he soon came around and encouraged me to keep fighting to go back to school. When that day happened, he was so happy for me. He was at my college graduation early and if you allowed him to tell it, he wanted the world to know that his sister beat all odds and that I came out as a winner!

Charley V.

Charley V. is my third oldest brother. He is the one that is quite different from the rest. He was the brother that everybody identified as good looking. He had an air about him that ignited his quiet personality. This air intrigued people especially the women. They wanted to know who he was and where did he come from? All those good looks charm, and so-called quiet sprit, landed him three sons before he finished High School.

Charley was quite different indeed. He would not hurt a fly; he never criticized anyone; he would give you the shirt off his back and yet he was probably more hurt than all my family members because he could not offer any advice to me when I got pregnant because he did not lead out by example.

I remember one of the girls that was pregnant by him - her name was Linda Ray. Linda's parents were the owners and operators of the only Black nursing care facility in Hugo. Linda, her sister, Ada, and I were great friends. I spent many nights in their home in the country. One particular weekend we were allowed to go out, but we had a time limit to get home. Of course Linda was dating Charlie, and I was just hoping that I could just have fun being out. Ada was always different - she would play all the way to the edge of the water but she would never stick her foot in the water. - that is while nobody was looking.

Linda was late getting back to the designated area and Ada was very upset because she knew that the keys were going to be taken and they were going to be grounded in the country. I think this was one of the first times I actually started my ministry because I told them that the only way that we were going to be able to get out of this situation was that we were going to have to get on our knees and say the 23ʳᵈ Psalms (The Lord is my Shepherd) 6 times each and that all would be well. You talking about some praying soul sisters - that's what we were that night. Well God is faithful. Mrs. Ray fussed a little bit but we were not in trouble.

Linda was so very kind to me. She bought me dresses and she invited me to go with her to her huge piano recital at Hugo High School. I got the opportunity to turn the pages for her while she played. I felt so special that night. Linda and I spent a lot of time together, but she and Charley never married. Charlie, however, kept his belief in me. In spite of my situation, he knew deep down inside that I was going to have to raise my son without his father just as the other girls who had children by him. Charlie was always there if I needed to share my heart. He knew how to listen; he just allowed me to vent and he smiled occasionally and after I was finished, I felt better. He always supported me in everything in his quiet way. I thank God for Charley because he taught me how to take the lumps and just go through. His favorite saying was "it will be all right in the morning".

Kenneth Craig

Kenneth Craig was my fourth oldest brother but he was only three years older than I was we were best buds. Kenneth was so very different from the rest of us. He used to love the Beatles and his favorite songs were Baby-Baby, Can't you Hear My Heart Beat, and She Loves Me Yeah-yeah-yeah. On one hand, we thought that he was crazy, but I also thought he was the greatest. Kenneth spent most of his time concentrating on how to get me in trouble so I could get a whipping. He used to love to pick the switches for Mother. He would trim them perfectly so that when Mother started whipping, the switch would not break. After my whipping was over, he would be in the shadows lurking and laughing or mocking how I acted trying to run away from Mother.

In spite of all that, I still had great fun with Kenneth. After the older siblings left home, Kenneth was the next in charge. Kenneth used to hate it when Mother and Daddy would go visit our uncles and aunts because he knew he was going to have to baby sit us. His motto was, "since I have to babysit, I am going to make everybody in the house obey me." He would have Debra and me boxing each other. He would wet our faces and dab them with a towel and introduce us to our little brother, Tony. He would say, "In this corner we have Joe Lewis, and in this corner we have Cassius Clay", and he would put us in the ring. I would start out wind-milling and Debra would wait until I was tired and with one punch I was out for the count. I would start crying as though I was being beat to death, but I would always go back for more.

There were other times that Kenneth and I would take some old mix-match socks to wear on our hands for gloves and we would ice skate in the bridge by our house for hours. Sometimes I would want to follow Kenneth and he would want to go play with the Bills', so he would rock me all the way home. There is another incident that sticks out in my mind when I think about Kenneth – he told Debra and me that he had a dish he wanted us to try. He said it would be a dish that we would never forget so we took the dish that looked like green beans but it had green peppers mixed in them. We took one bite and our mouths burned within - we kept trying to drink water to cool our tongues but nothing worked and he laughed until he cried.

Kenneth was always the life of the family and he had wisdom beyond his years. The only time that he really irritated me was when I became pregnant. I was so hurt I could not tell him because we did everything together and now I would not be able to do all the fun things we used to do. When Kenneth found out I was pregnant, he was totally hurt but he never let on to me. He continued to meddle me as though nothing had changed and I was grateful for that. Kenneth was a senior in High School when I had Kerwin. It was a sad time for both of us because he went on to college and I did not get a chance to see him much but he always wanted to know how Kerwin and I were doing. Whenever he came home, he started teasing Kerwin. I knew that was his way of saying its okay.

The only real advice that I can distinctly remember Kenneth ever giving me was, "Marsha, you do not want to stay in Hugo. You need to graduate, go on to college and you will have a much better life". I took his advice and pursued my education. I ended up at the University where he was attending; his friends became my friends, and his best friend became my husband. The day his diploma came in the mail inspired me to complete my education. I thank God for Kenneth and his ability to touch my life the way that he did. It has truly generated a lifelong bond between us even to this day. My best bud - Kenneth Craig.

Debrah Joyce

Debra Joyce was the sister who was two years younger than I was. She was always on the go. Debra wasn't happy unless she was going somewhere. She would just think about someone and she would leave. Debra was always head-strong and stubborn. Once Debra made up her mind about a thing, wild horses could not stop her from doing what she wanted to do. Even though I am the oldest, Debra always thought of me as being boring. She never wanted to do anything with me because I was always trying to get her not to do something that she really wanted to do. She discovered at an early age that if she wanted to do what she wanted to do, her best bet was to leave me at home.

Debra had the cutest dimples and the prettiest smile. She was very athletic and she was selected to be a varsity cheerleader when she was only a freshman. She was a great softball player and could drive a car better than most. She was known for her french-fried potatoes which always came out golden brown. We used to argue day and night with each other, but something happened when I became pregnant. When Debra found out, her entire demeanor changed. She was much kinder to me and in spite of all that was happening, she would allow me to try on her clothes that Bernice had bought her knowing that I could not wear any of them. I know that she would not have allowed me to even look at her clothes if I had not been pregnant. She never said a word about my being pregnant but at school if she heard one negative word, she would always defend her big sister even though I was pregnant. She would keep me abreast of everything that was going on at school. When Kerwin was born, Debra was like the rest of my siblings, she fell in love with Kerwin and did her part by playing, hugging, and kissing him. I know she felt bad for me, but she always made me feel better. We became much closer in our relationship and she did everything within her power to make things easier for me and Kerwin.

Tony Lydell

Tony Lydell, my big little brother, is also my baby brother who was born on the last day of school. There was a lot of commotion going on that day - Arbrey's dog "Sports", and Mama Mag's dog "Old Boy" were fighting a black cat that hung around our house to catch the rats. I was terrified of the rats - they were in the creek by our house. One day we heard all of this barking and cat meow's and all of a sudden the dogs were pulling on the cat until the cat 's head went one way and the tail went the other way. I was so happy because I was terrified of that black cat with those green eyes.

Shortly after that event we were greeted by the neighbor, Mrs. Verna Mae Jackson, who had made a big pot of stew and cornbread and instructed us to be very quiet because we had a new baby brother. Mrs. Verna Mae gave us the okay from mother who allowed us to come in and take a look at him. When we arrived home, he was there big and strong, and was just as cute as a button. All the older siblings had an opportunity to try and name him. Charley wanted him named Patrick; Arbrey wanted him named Michael Eugene after him; Bernice wanted him named Tony Kenneth like Rydell for a middle name so they ended up naming him Tony Lydell and we were all happy campers.

Tony was a happy baby. He grew by leaps and bounds so much so that he outgrew all my other brothers and was much larger in body structure. Tony used to love watching the Three Stooges. He would get up early in the morning and watch them while everyone else was asleep. We always knew what he had been doing because he would imitate them all day long. Tony was a gentle giant who loved to eat and boy could he eat! He would eat all the food you put in front of him even in his high chair. He always wanted more.

Eventually it caught up with him because he became bigger, stronger, and taller than anyone in the family.

Tony love picking Daddy up off the floor. He was an obedient little brother, and was always trying to be helpful. We discovered that when I had Kerwin, Tony was only ten years old, the same age I was when mother had her last baby, Lori Ann.

Tony was much too young in my opinion to hold Kerwin but he always wanted to. When I would go outside to hang up Kerwin's clothes on the clothes line, Tony would sneak in the bedroom where Kerwin was laying and he would pick him up and hold him. I could always tell because when I entered the room, the bed would still be moving because he had to hurry and put him back on the bed before I came in the room. Tony was a good little brother and helped me by getting Kerwin's bottles. He would play with Kerwin when I allowed him, but he was too young to understand my struggles and my pain. He knew that Kerwin was my son, and that he was an uncle so all was well with him. Tony is still the uncle who gets more respect than all the rest because he is not just my big little brother, he is also the big little Uncle.

Lori Ann

Lori Ann Akins - this is It! She is the last of the Akins children. Lori was a beautiful baby but I could not believe that mother was still having children and I was in the fifth grade. Well she did, and immediately, Lori became my responsibility. I hated having to feed her and change her diapers while mother was preparing dinner. I especially hated having to take her with me when I wanted to go play in the *Belmont*.

Mother was such a drill sergeant. She would make this long list of do's and don'ts when it came to her baby. I remember one time when I was feeding Lori some baby food from the jar I had heated up in a pot on the wood stove, I hurriedly took the top off when prunes began to spill out of the jar due to pressure build up. The food was warm on my legs so I started screaming Prunes popped! prunes popped! Mother came and checked everything out. After she realized I was okay, she made me go right back to the task at hand. Lori was a cute girl and she was always quiet, and I finally grew very fond of her.

When Kerwin was born, Lori was 6 years old, so she really did not understand that he was her nephew. She was just excited to have a baby in the house. Lori was always wanting to hold Kerwin and play with him, but I was a very over- protective mother, so it was not often that I was in the mind set to let her hold him. When I did let her hold Kerwin, she cherished the moments. Lori loved him and thought he was the next best thing to ice cream.

As the years went by, Lori, like Tony, grew up to be very tall. She surpassed all of us in height. She looks exactly like my mother. When I finally left home with Kerwin, Lori was very sad to see me leave because Kerwin was more like a little brother to her than her nephew. All in all, Lori was a good little sister and she helped out with Kerwin by washing his soiled diapers, bringing his bottles to me, and playing with him as much as I would allow her. Lori declares to this day that I always promised to bring her a treat from the store and that she is still waiting for it.

Chapter 24

I Missed A Step, But I Caught Up

24 _I Missed A Step, But I Caught Up_

Wow! What a Journey? Thank you for taking the time to walk through the **Belmont Addition** Open House with me. As you can see, my life is an open book for all to read. Certainly you recognized the house that was once shattered and disheveled. I know that as you entered the door into our home, you were able to recognize the knob that was chipped and cracked by the broken experiences of childhood anguish, anxiety, and disappointment. The glorious part about this experience is that all of the rough edges were smoothed out by a measure of time, distance, and love.

Splattered on the walls were hurts that are now healed. I know that you were able to feel the humility that hung from the ceiling as you walked from room to room. In the doorways, disappointments used to block the entry way, but perseverance caused them to no longer linger there. In our living room, I hope you were able to experience life and that more abundantly. Tell me, when you entered the kitchen, were you able to feast at our table which was overlaid with kindness?

As you walked into the bathroom, did you notice how white washed the walls were? At one time they were covered with bitterness. In the master bedroom, did you notice peace, prosperity, and purpose lying on the bed?

Down through the years our home became more than a place to me, it became my struggles, my security, and my hope. It is the spot that reminded me that no matter what I went through, I could always go back to the *Belmont* to get a refreshing and start all over again. This place taught me not to despise small beginnings. It also germinated within me a sense of realness, integrity and honesty.

The footprints of my predecessors gave me direction and motivated my hope. In addition, it provided me with the building blocks of fortitude and perseverance which enabled me to continue on no matter how difficult it seemed. The *Addition* itself is a place that will forever be embedded in the corridors of my mind, in the crevices of my soul, and in every fiber of my being.

To each of you who have shared my trials, and to the remainder of you who have rejoiced in my triumphs, thank you. I know that we crossed some patches that were filled with stickers, but you made it through with me. Mere words cannot express how grateful I am to God for giving me the opportunity to accomplish another milestone in my life. This book was birthed in my sprit based on my memory from four years of age forward. I believe that God ordained my life to go in print while I was still in my mother's womb.

It was my heart's desire to complete this book by March 2007 because the number 7 represents completion. I am also my father's 7th child and I will be 52 years old on March 28, 2007. If you add the numbers 5 and 2 together, you get 7!

My purpose for sharing my story is to let the world know that even though I missed a step, I caught up. Though my trials were many, my time was in God's hand. Although I was not able to release all of my tears of pain, rejection, hurt and disappointment during the times of my growth and development, I have now been able to release tears of refreshing, tears of joy, and tears of release as I wrote my story.

I have further shared my story as a source of hope for every parent who has become tired and tempted to give up on their children, for the families who are experiencing division and strife, for every young girl who must wear the banner of having a baby out of wedlock. I speak to you now and say, "Stop, reach down on the inside of your inner being and pull out change" - Welcome it, Wear it, and Walk in it. Trust God to renew, reform, and revive you.

I hope you can now see that I am the *Belmont Addition* and the *Belmont Addition* is who I am. Even today, the *Belmont Addition* continues to impact my life and will continue to do so for the rest of my life!!

Reference

IN THE DISTRICT COURT OF CHOCTAW COUNTY,
STATE OF OKLAHOMA

Marsha Jo Akins, a minor, by and through her mother and
next friend, Bobbie Jean Akins,

                              Plaintiff,
VS,

Simon Parker, Morris Upchurch, and the Board of Education
of Independent School District Number 39 of Choctaw
County, Oklahoma,

                              Defendant,
NO.C-72-139

FILED
IN DISTRICT COURT
CHOCTAW COUNTY, OKLA
11-22-72

Reference

IN THE DISTRICT COURT IN AND FOR CHOCTAW
COUNTY, OKLHOMA

MARSHA JO AKINS,   PLAINTIFF,

Vs.

Simon Parker   DEFENDANT

N0.c-72-139
ORDER OF DISMISSAL

Now on this the 24th day of May, 1973, the above cause
is dismissed by the Court for lack of prosecution without
prejudice to the filing of another action.

Neal Merriot, District Judge

FILED

IN DISTRICT COURT
CHOCTAW COUNTY, OKLA.
5-25-73
Opal Henderson
By Jody Yandell

Printed in the United States
80113LV00004B/133-270